Adoniram Judson

Adoniram Judson

Edited by Faith Coxe Bailey

MOODY PRESS
CHICAGO

© 1955, by
THE MOODY BIBLE INSTITUTE
OF CHICAGO

ISBN: 0-8024-0287-9

13 15 17 19 20 18 16 14 12

Printed in the United States of America

CONTENTS

94996

Chapter One

AN ATHEIST IN THE PARSONAGE

WHEN HE WAS ABOUT TEN YEARS OLD, Adoniram Judson stole off into a quiet corner of the family house at Wenham, Massachusetts, and, licking the end of his pencil thoughtfully, produced the solution to a ticklish puzzle printed in the local newspaper. Instead of the prize offered by the paper for this solution, he was embarrassed at the family supper table for his giddiness. His taciturn, authoritarian father gave him a look of complete rejection and punishment, and a book of arithmetic so that he might put his puzzle-solving turn of mind to a more profitable use!

That more profitable use proved to be a gigantic puzzle that had never been solved by any man, a riddle that took twenty-seven years to untangle! With his love of details, and that love multiplied by dedication to God's work, Adoniram Judson solved his greatest puzzle—the translation of the English Bible into Burmese. Today Burmese men and women find the answer to the riddle of life from this translation which still stands, more than a hundred years later, as the best of its kind.

Adoniram's searchings began early and were seldom appreciated by those nearest and dearest to him. One day he failed to turn up for the noonday meal. His father set out to look for him. Axioms regarding the

7

promptness, the obedience, and the place of small children occupied the paternal mind as did the search for a suitable willow twig and his son. He found Adoniram without much trouble, flat on his back in the meadow, an old felt hat covering his ruddy face and most of his copper-colored curls.

"Sir, what's the meaning of this?" his father thundered, yanking small Adoniram to his feet.

"Just looking at the sun, sir," Adoniram said vaguely, standing up and blinking at his father with swollen, bloodshot, runny eyes. He was promptly hustled off to what usually awaited small New England boys after such a daring piece of disobedience. But to his sister Adoniram whispered, "It does move, I saw it." The trip to the meadow had been an important scientific search; someone had told Adoniram that the earth revolved around the sun, but he didn't see how this could be. His restless mind wasn't content until he knew whether or not the sun really moved. His morning in the meadow answered the question—at least to his seven-year-old satisfaction!

Born in Malden, Massachusetts, in 1788, and moving, as his minister-father changed parishes, to Wenham, Braintree, and Plymouth, Adoniram Judson was never farther from Boston than a carriage ride. He grew up in an atmosphere as cultured, refined, and proper as a Beacon Hill home. His father was a Congregational minister, and someone has left this apt description: "His white hair, erect posture, grave utterance, and somewhat taciturn manner, left one somewhat at a loss whether to class him with the patriarchs of the Hebrews or the censors of the Romans." Adoniram's mother was a gentlewoman, polished in speech, correct in manners, and probably as thoroughly frightened by the domineering position her husband took in the household as were the Judson children. Adoniram's sister, Abigail, was a year and a half younger than he, Elnathan, six years younger.

From the moment that Pastor Judson knew he had a son, he was convinced of one thing: the boy was to be great, famous, eminent. When he returned from a preaching mission, and the three-year-old child toddled up to him and proceeded to read an entire chapter from the Bible, the elder Judson was certain his hopes were to be realized. That young Don gathered neighborhood children around him and preached to them, when he was only four, was triumphantly recorded in the Judson family records.

Determined that his son aim for greatness, the stern clergyman gave him the best education available—a strange potpourri of teachers and subjects. When Adoniram was ten, he was hustled off to a retired Plymouth sea captain. The captain quite naturally taught Adoniram the subject he knew best—navigation. Plymouth, the country's first village, boasted a grammar school. When Adoniram transferred here, he mastered the Greek language at the age of twelve. Did he mind when other fellows mocked his prowess, and because of an old felt hat he was attached to, called him "old Vergil dug up"?

When he was sixteen, he entered Brown University, a full year ahead of most, convincing someone besides his father he was indeed destined for great things. This other person was—Adoniram himself.

If he could enter one of the oldest, finest universities

in all of this new country, what couldn't he do? He could be an orator, or a poet, or even a statesman, leading hundreds of people in this wonderful, brave democracy. He would be famous, rich. Extravagant ambition spiraled up and up, and then, suddenly in his imagination he knew why Alexander had wept. Where could he go from the top? Would people forget him a hundred years from now? Maybe he'd insure greater fame if he were a clergyman—not a parish preacher like his father, but an eminent, learned philosophical divine.

He gloated over this brand of success for awhile—the finest carriage in town, the whitest house on Main street, perhaps a pulpit in Boston eventually. He was vaguely uneasy about a minister who worked at success, but he pushed the uneasiness out of his mind. Adoniram didn't want to look too deeply into his own heart these years; he didn't want to admit to himself that he wasn't a Christian and that he wasn't particularly anxious to become one.

The university campus was merely a rough field, about eight acres, overlooking the sea and the city of Providence. But here Adoniram was introduced to a world quite foreign to the somber, sedate Congregational parsonage. It was a world of rivals as quick-witted as he, and of new friends who talked in different accents and thought new daring thoughts.

To the rivals Adoniram adjusted quite simply. He studied harder, worked later, and topped them in the final score. The week before commencement it was a nip-and-tuck race with a young chap named John Bailey (later a Massachusetts congressman) and Adoniram. Finally, the marks were in. The announcement was made. Valedictorian of the class of seventeen was— A. Judson. The exulting note Adoniram wrote home makes it plain he hadn't lost his dream of success. "Dear Father, I have got it."

Handling his new friends with their exciting, strange ideas was more difficult. A chap who swore he didn't believe in God—what could he and Adoniram, brought up in a Bible-centered parsonage, have in common? The truth was they had much in common—their ambition, their quick wit, their flair for the dramatic, their love for studying. How many oil lamps flickered out while Adoniram and his new friend, this chap called E———, debated future careers, politics, and again and again, philosophy!

Perhaps Adoniram protested strongly at first against Voltaire and his colleagues of French infidelity, calling back as arguments sermons he'd heard his father preach. But finally, his arguments grew feebler and feebler. E———, with his witty repartee and his agile logic, had won. The two friends didn't debate any longer, they discussed, for they were both on the same side of the question. Adoniram made no pretense of hiding from anyone that he considered himself—a declared atheist!

After graduation, and after a one-year adventure as headmaster of an academy for young ladies, Adoniram returned home, determined to leave immediately on a five- or six-hundred mile trip, a trip aimed purely at pleasure and getting to know some of the world he'd never seen. He also determined not to hide matters from his family any more. Why should they think he was still the same immature, God-fearing youngster?

His statement of his totally atheistic philosophy to his father and mother stunned them, but only for a moment. Then his mother broke into gentle sobs, while his father roared and threatened and pounded on the parsonage furniture. The older Judson expostulated every logic he could cull from his mind; but it was of no use. Adoniram's mind, fresh from university, was too agile. He convinced himself he was leaps ahead of his father.

He left that afternoon on his jaunt. His excitement over reaching Albany and witnessing the marvel of the year, the Robert Fulton steamer, drove the distasteful memory of his father's argument out of his mind. But somehow, even the lovely fields and trees of western Massachusetts could not distract him from remembering his mother's tears!

Chapter Two

THE MIRACLE OF THE
ONLY ROOM LEFT

TO THE TWENTY-ONE-YEAR-OLD preacher's son from
New England, Robert Fulton's exciting new invention seemed like the fastest—and the most exciting—way
into the exotic life he was determined to explore. As
the "Clermont," magnificently belching black smoke, its
rear paddles churning the Hudson wildly, headed for
New York City, Adoniram Judson knew he was right.
The scenery—sharp embankments, distant mountains—
was delightfully foreign to his seacoast eyes, and more
wonderful than that, nobody aboard ship suspected he
was a preacher's son. Somebody picked up his name as
Johnson—the name of a popular novelist! Adoniram saw
no reason in disappointing so many admiring new
friends by telling them his name was pronounced Judson.

New York, in the early 1800's, was asparkle with
sailors jabbering strange tongues, prosperous merchants
in high silk hats, buildings clustered around the center
of the island, and a strange new after-dark life that
fascinated the wide-eyed country boy. This was the
theater, aglitter with witty plays, beautiful young wom-
en, and companions who shrugged off the cares of
tomorrow by living well today. Adoniram joined a
theatrical company—a stock company that specialized
in melodrama, high living, and some dubious financial

practices, such as skipping out of rooming houses without paying the landlord!

And why not? He approached this new life with an open mind. For about a year Adoniram reveled in New York's sophistication.

Then his friends began to chatter intriguingly about the West. Footloose Adoniram decided to sample life out there too. His horse, his only transportation, he had left in the barn attached to Uncle Ephraim's Sheffield, Connecticut, parsonage. Adoniram left New York City for Sheffield.

After New York's glitter the Congregational parsonage seemed dark and musty. His uncle was away, and Adoniram spent that evening making an effort at conversation with the young preacher who was his substitute—offensively pious, Adoniram thought. The conversation caught on a hook of religion, godliness, and theology, and Adoniram tried to jerk it away, unsuccessfully. He went to bed bored and irritated; he rode off next morning thoroughly disgruntled.

The fresh air, as his horse trotted west, blew away the annoying memories of a dull evening. The excitement of exploring the West returned; that evening, in a relaxed, pleasant mood, he turned his horse into a traveler's inn for the night. But the man behind the wooden counter shattered his mood when he said,

"You'll forgive me, sir, but the only room left—well, it'll be a bit noisy. There's a young fellow next door awful sick."

"I'm tired enough to sleep anywhere through anything."

"He might—be dying, the doctor says. You don't mind —the noise—or—being that close."

"My good fellow, I trust I'm old enough and wise enough so that a stranger's dying doesn't frighten me. Just hand over my key."

But the night was a nightmare. In the beginning only the tramp, tramp of the doctor's feet, the occasional scrape of a chair on the wooden floor, the constant mumble of voices, kept him awake. But then he began to think—someone was dying in the next room! What of that—people died every day! But this was a young man—we all die eventually. But was he ready? What would happen to him the instant his heart stopped? What a puerile, fearful thought! His father wouldn't say so! But how his good friend E—— would snicker! *He'd* have an answer for this infantile, emotional feeling—an intellectual, rational answer. His father would have an answer too. Maybe this young fellow had a Christian father.

Next morning Adoniram wearily pushed his key across the wooden counter. "How'd ya sleep?" the clerk asked.

"Extraordinarily badly." As an afterthought he asked, "How's the young chap?"

"I thought maybe you would have heard—when they took him out, I mean. He died, sir, toward morning it was."

"A shame," Adoniram turned away, hesitated. "He was young, you say?"

"Very young. Just out of school, I figure. Not more than your age. Went to that there Brown University out East."

"Brown Uni—I might have known him! What was his name?"

"His name, sir? I don't know as I can tell. Wait a minute, I have the records. Here we are. His name was E——, sir!"

It took a minute for Adoniram to understand what the desk clerk had said. His friend E—— was dead. The chap who had all the answers knew now that those answers were wrong. E—— was lost! Perhaps it wasn't until he mounted his horse and was automatically heading west that Adoniram realized the implication of that thought. In his heart he believed that E—— was lost. And that meant one thing: this whole way of life he was so deliberately carving out for himself, all of its superficiality, its dishonesty, was wrong!

The West lost its lure, and Adoniram Judson turned his horse's head eastward and started off at a gallop for Plymouth. Reaching home, he announced to his startled parents that he was going to enter a theological school.

There were three obstacles to Adoniram's entrance, and all of them put in the way by the school itself— Andover, a Congregational school in eastern Massachusetts. He didn't qualify for advanced work, for he wasn't a theological professor. Nor did he want to prepare for the ministry. The third reason? Adoniram Judson wasn't even ready to admit he was a Christian!

The teachers, who voted finally to admit him, soon realized how wise they were. Adoniram discovered that Old Testament history, Paul's conversion, and the Sermon on the Mount were as dramatic as the New York stage. The doctrine of the atonement, the Trinity, the virgin birth, were as satisfying to a philosophical mind as Voltaire! .Within three months, he had dedicated his life to Christ; in December, 1808, he accepted Him as his Saviour. Six months later, in June, 1809, for the first time in his life, he became a church member, joining the Congregational church which his father pastored.

He had a new Master, he was a new creature, and everything in life he determined to judge in a new way. You would have known it the minute you stepped into his tidy dormitory room, with its even stacks of paper, its dustless bookcases. Small signs, carefully printed by hand, were tacked up everywhere in the room. "I put them where I will be most apt to see them on things I look at every day or use most often," Adoniram explained. The signs probed every thought, every decision. They read, "Is it pleasing to God?"

"Say, Judson, here's a book you must read," a fellow-theologue told him one night.

"With examinations looming up, you want me to read books?"

The chap held out a slim volume. "Only a small one. It's a sermon more than anything. By a chap named Claude Buchanan."

"Buchanan?"

"Used to be chaplain of the British East India Company—or still is, I don't know. But what he says about what the Gospel's done for those heathen, well, it'll thrill you."

Adoniram Judson borrowed the thin book, a book called *The Star of the East,* written by the chaplain of the company which ironically was to persecute and hound him so cruelly. Not knowing how this book would change his whole life, he began to read.

His first wild enthusiasm—"Surely this is where I must go, what I must do, the people I must preach to"— was followed by cramping doubts: "A wild chase, how could I get there, wouldn't I die of some tropic fever?" He plunged into a full-scale battle within himself. He talked to his professors, he prayed. He could not, no matter how hard he tried, forget the message of his little book—men were saved from eternal damnation because some brave folks risked everything to preach to them. Next he read, *Embassy to Ava,* a tale of heroic adventure with the Gospel in Burma. At one moment he knew he was called to India. The next, he wasn't sure.

Even in the woods in back of the seminary he found no peace of mind. Plodding over the stubby grass, sitting, head in hands, on a fallen tree trunk, Adoniram fought the thing out. He lifted his eyes toward the White Mountains in the North. "From whence cometh my help," he quoted. For the time, no help came. He prayed, he listened, he debated.

The book had talked to him; he heard God's voice saying, "Preach my Word in India." But if it really was God, would He have stopped speaking and left this awful silence? Adoniram picked up a leaf from the muddy ground, twirled it endlessly around and around, then dropped it. As swiftly as a wet leaf falls to the ground, his answer came. "Go ye into all the world and preach the gospel." He heard it as clearly as if someone had spoken. And that was it, of course. Someone did speak, and on that day in February, 1810, Adoniram

Judson dedicated his life to the salvation of the East!

But after he battled through to his decision, was Adoniram lonesome with it? His professors were teaching either practical parish techniques or involved theology. Samuel Nott, another student, talked missions with Adoniram, but he must have been the only one. Perhaps Adoniram wondered how lonely India would be if he felt so alone in the midst of a Christian seminary!

And then the Haystackers arrived, four new students just graduated from Williams College. Adoniram discovered he wasn't alone. These four young men shared his dream—they had consecrated themselves to the mission field beneath a gigantic haystack on the Williams College farm! Together the six stalwart young men prayed, planned, and talked about the future. They saw themselves clearly as six men sent by God to save thousands halfway around the world!

But well-meaning folk had other ideas about Adoniram's lifework! As he finished his seminary work (he graduated in June, 1810), he saw several plums dangling in front of him. He could teach at his alma mater: Brown University promised him a tempting tutor's appointment. He turned it down. Dr. Griffin invited him to share his pulpit, the biggest, richest one in Boston; Adoniram could have his adolescent dream of that carriage and impressive parsonage in the finest cultural environment in the New World! But Boston bored Adoniram.

"You'll be so near home," his mother pleaded.

He had an answer. "I'll never live in Boston. I've much farther to go!"

One serious obstacle remained for him, Samuel Nott, and the Haystackers, and it was all summed up in the definition of a word. When the six friends looked for a board to support their mission to the East, they were dismayed. Adoniram was inspired to preach to the Saviourless men and women in India; the only missionary society in the entire country, the Massachusetts Missionary Society, was formed to carry the Gospel to *Indians,* true—but they were the American Indians!

Chapter Three

A VISIONARY TAKES ACTION

"IT SEEMS TO ME that you young gentlemen are extraordinarily visionary!" Andover's Professor Stuart remarked, as he stirred his tea slowly, deliberately. Five tense young seminary students sat in a row on the huge overstuffed sofa under the mantel. Across the room, gripping the curved arms of a Windsor chair, Adoniram Judson leaned forward and said in an even tone, "Visionary? because we want to preach the Gospel halfway around the world?"

Professor Stuart flicked the handle of his teacup with his thumb nail. "Seems to me, young Judson, I hear a great deal from the six of you about preaching the Gospel across the globe. But I hear nothing about what you are doing here to get there!"

Adoniram jumped to his feet, and as he paced, his deep, throaty voice boomed out, "Do! What can we do! There isn't a missionary society in the whole country that's ready to think about sending preachers across the sea yet. They're still thinking about *this* country as a mission field. Ridiculous! With our strong new government in Washington, our president, our states, and churches in every one of them, mind you—us, a mission field!"

Professor Stuart continued to flick his teacup handle.

Adoniram went on. "I'll tell you what we did, Professor Stuart. We wrote a letter to England, straight to the London Missionary Society, asking them to support us!"

"Courage to write letters, and dream dreams, yes. But what about courage to go to a man face to face and say to him, 'Brother, will you pay for my food and clothing and doctor bills so that I can obey God's call?'"

"Courage to ask a man! *What* man, Professor Stuart?"

"Tomorrow our General Association of Congregational Churches in New England convenes at Bradford, ten miles away. You can walk it easily, Judson, if you want to. There'll be men there to ask."

"You mean—"

"I mean that if you young gentlemen mean to get to India, you won't dream any more dreams and you won't waste any more time waiting for slow-moving British friends to answer. You'll draw up a petition, ask for support, sign your names, and present that petition at tomorrow's meeting."

Somebody found a quill, Professor Stuart produced the paper, and the petition was scratched out in a fury of hopefulness. " . . . They now offer the following inquiries, on which they solicit the opinion and advice of this Association: Whether, with their present views and feelings, they ought to renounce the object of missions, as either visionary or impracticable; if not, whether they ought to direct their attention to the eastern or western world; whether they may expect patronage and support from a missionary society in this country."

In a rambling scrawl, Judson signed first, then Samuel Nott, Samuel Mills, Samuel Newell, Luther Rice, and James Richards took the quill. Would six names— six men to guarantee support—frighten the association away? Cautiously, and reluctantly, a line was drawn through Rice and Richards!

If Adoniram Judson, striding over the fields the next day, his nervous hands growing icier, and the dull ache in his stomach heavier at every half-mile, expected a clear-cut *yes*, or even a clear-cut *no*, from the General Association, he was bitterly disappointed. The august, austere gathering listened respectfully to the reading of the petition. They debated, discussed, prayed, debated, discussed, and argued some more. The young seminary students, led by the most zealous and courageous Mr. Judson, were undoubtedly sincere, dedicated, called by God. The foreign mission field was a worthy cause. Finally, the association appointed nine men to form the highly official-sounding American Board of Commissioners for Foreign Missions.

But it was a strangely timid board. The resolution said, weakly and inconclusively, "We advise the young gentlemen, whose request is before us, in the way of earnest prayer and diligent attention to suitable studies and means of information, and putting themselves under the patronage and direction of the Board, humbly to wait for openings and guidance of Providence in respect to their great and excellent design." What the Board was saying between the lines was this: the New England churches were definitely too new, too weak to underwrite such a quixotic and speculative venture!

The Board made one concrete suggestion: ask some-one for financial help! England's well-established churches were a logical choice. The London Missionary Society had adequate funds. The American Board of Commissioners voted to ask for help in supporting its missionaries to India.

When Adoniram headed his horse back toward Andover, two thoughts fought for first place in his mind. The first—he was elected to argue his case before the London Missionary Society in person, sailing to England as soon as passage could be booked. The second thought—a vivid memory of the day's dinner at the Hasseltine home.

Yet, actually, he couldn't remember the dinner at all. From the minute Ann Hasseltine walked into the dining-room to serve the table of ministers, Adoniram was completely unaware of what he was eating. He uneasily recalled his inane conversation to the men seated on either side of him. And what an oaf Ann herself must have thought him! He was so engrossed in composing a sonnet to her long, brown curls she asked twice for his dinner plate!

Ann Hasseltine! He knew she must be about his age, that she was the youngest daughter of Congregational deacon, John Hasseltine, that she was the gayest girl in all Bradford, and that she was truly lovely!

It took six months to book young Judson's passage to London. Did the six months' delay, which meant, of course, six months' delay in arriving on any mission field, really disappoint him? Or did frequent trips to Bradford soothe his impatience?

In this six months' time, Adoniram courted Ann Hasseltine with as much confidence as if he'd been a Boston banker, instead of a practically penniless seminary student, without even a missionary's meager allowance guaranteed him yet! He was fully aware that never before had a white woman gone from North America as a missionary to India. He must have heard that the Bradford neighbors gossiped, "I'd tie my daughter to a bedpost before I'd allow her to be a missionary's wife!"

In spite of everything, he wrote the letter that concluded his business in Bradford. "I have now to ask whether you can consent to part with your daughter, whether you can consent to her departure to a heathen land, and her subjection to the hardships and sufferings of a missionary life? Whether you can consent to her exposure to the dangers of the ocean, to the fatal influence of the southern climate of India, to every kind of want and distress, to degradation, insult, persecution, and perhaps a violent death!"

Fortunately John Hasseltine did not listen very long to neighborhood gossip. He was a real Christian. His Nancy had won him and her mother to her Saviour. By the time Adoniram sailed for England, he and Ann were engaged.

January, 1811, just one short year before the irritated outburst of the War of 1812, was hardly a wise time to cross the Atlantic in an English vessel. The "Packet," on which Adoniram sailed, was a plucky little ship, but not stout enough to ward off the menacing French privateers that accosted and captured her a few days out.

At gunpoint Adoniram was ordered onto the deck of the "L'Invincible Napoleon." His frantic explanation of who he was and what his business was brought only shrugs and snickers from the French crew. He could speak no French. For safe measure, he was chucked into the dingy, sour-smelling hold of the boat, as it veered away from London, headed toward France!

After two days of violent seasickness in the airless, filthy hold, with no one to understand him if he asked for a drink of water, Adoniram questioned his whole errand. What was he, a refined, cultured, well-educated gentleman, doing here, treated like an animal, lying in a heap of dirty straw! He was Adoniram Judson, who had been offered the biggest church in Boston. If only he'd accepted and forgotten this foolishness.

In the midst of his lonely self-pity, he remembered God. His head reeling, his stomach lurching, he tried to pray. By the time the privateer docked in Bayonne, France, Adoniram was resigned, for God had given him an answer. This misery must be endured because God was preparing him for even greater torment ahead —in His service.

But in Bayonne, humiliation was heaped on his misery. With the "Packet" crew, he was marched along the street, while villagers jeered. If only he knew enough French to make someone understand who he was! Clutching at the few words he knew, he flung them out. A ragged youngster laughed. Giggle at his American pronunciation, would he? Maybe he'd get more attention if he gave a volley of English!

"Oppression is the curse of the world. These men oppress me. They detain me against my will. It is an offense against me and my country and . . . " he bellowed.

"Lower your voice."

"You talk English!" Adoniram tried to twist his head to spot the man in the street crowd.

"Yes, and I advise you to keep your thoughts to yourself."

"Who are you?"

"An American from Philadelphia."

"Then help me!"

"If you keep your voice down."

"I will be a perfect lamb. All I wanted was attention and I have it—"

"Go to jail. That's where they'll take you. Do what they say. Don't argue. I'll be there to help you."

The straw in the jail was matted with years of filth. The stench made Adoniram's eyes water. He, who demanded clean linen every day, who never left a book out of line on his bookshelves, was expected to stay— even an hour—here! He leaned against a column—he wouldn't sit down—and shuddered! In Boston he might be sipping tea in a cozy Beacon Hill drawing-room now.

At the end of a tormented night the American came, sweeping through the door with a gigantic cape thrown over his shoulder. He looked around once, twice, declared that none of these men were friends of his, poor devils, and then casually swung his great cloak over Adoniram! Some money in the palm of the astonished guard did the rest.

It took some maneuvering, but his Philadelphia friend managed to book his passage on a London-bound vessel. On the sixth of May, four months after he said good-bye to Ann Hasseltine, Adoniram's ship swung into the London harbor.

A low, thick fog hung over the city, and it seemed

to Adoniram as he docked that the fog and the misery of his tangle with the French was an omen of the outcome of his whole errand to Britain!

Chapter Four

"ANYTHING THEM
BRITISHERS CAN DO"

THE LONDON BUSINESS was quickly over. The London Missionary Society listened with grave attention to the eager, intense young American. They nodded with an understanding that smacked of patronage when he explained that churches in the brand-new United States of America weren't strong enough yet to support a foreign mission program.

Then they came up with an offer that topped what Adoniram had been instructed to ask for. The London Missionary Society volunteered to take over not half his support, but *all* of it, and to send him and the other young men to the mission field immediately as missionaries of the London Missionary Society!

There was only one condition. It was to be understood that Mr. Judson was completely and solely their missionary, that his action would not be dictated by any loyalty to the land of his birth.

Arriving back in Boston again the last of August, Adoniram had time for a quick visit at home, a quicker one at the Hasseltine's home on the banks of the river in Bradford, before he appeared before the September meeting of the Congregational church fathers, in the town of Worcester. To the American Board of Foreign Commissioners the boyish, slight, missionary-to-be stood up and announced his decision in his powerful, resonant voice. If the American society refused to take on his appointment singlehanded, he would become a missionary of the English society. Samuel Nott jumped up and declared the same resolution!

There was a sturdy ring of American independence in the reaction of the Congregational church fathers. So Britain refused to go halfway, even on a missionary enterprise! Well, the way affairs had gone in the last seventy-five years, it came as no surprise. Think the Americans would just sit back and let them grab the reins, did they? No, sir!

One of the Board laid his hand heavily on Adoniram's shoulders. "My boy," he said in his Yankee drawl, "reckon anything them Britishers can do, we can do! You—and your friend Nott, and Brother Newell and Brother Hall, too—you can consider your support guaranteed, by the Board. You'll go out as *American* missionaries—yes, sir!"

God was faithful; He opened the door to India. But when would Adoniram and Ann sail? The fall dragged by.

In January Samuel Newell and Gordon Hall sent a message from Philadelphia. In two weeks the ship "Harmony" sailed from that city to Calcutta, and the government permitted missionaries to book passage. Another war with England threatened; if they didn't sail immediately, the British might blockade ports and delay sailing for months even years!

On February 5, 1812, a hushed little handful of people collected in the west room of the Hasseltine home. Outside, a wicked wind spanked the Merrimac

River and wailed up along the valley. Harriet Atwood was there, Ann Hasseltine's shy, wistful friend. With her was Samuel Newell; later that week they would be married. Kindly old Pastor Allen, of the Bradford church, was there too, a little impatient to be on with the ceremony. Were some of the neighbors who had shaken their heads over Ann's frightful fate there, too?

Through the doorway stepped Ann, lithe, lovely in her long white wedding gown, to be married in the very room where she had first met Adoniram at the ministers' dinner. Standing before Pastor Allen, Ann and Adoniram heard him call them dear children, and bless them and their work with his benediction.

As his ordination was scheduled for the very next day, Adoniram hustled his new bride into the duties and demands of his calling. Probably she didn't complain; it was her calling, too.

It was bitterly cold in Salem that February 6, but the narrow, crooked streets of the seacoast town were crowded with people—all hustling to the white frame meeting house. Sleighs brought bundled, shivering families up from Boston. A few farmers galloped in on frothing horses. A delegation of students walked sixteen miles from Andover in the numbing cold of early morning.

Nobody wanted to miss this important event in the Congregational Church—the first foreign missionaries were to be ordained and commissioned!

Before the distinguished clergymen from Boston and other New England towns, Adoniram, Samuel Newell, Samuel Nott, Gordon Hall, and Luther Rice knelt. From a front row her wide eyes and pretty mouth partly hidden from the congregation by a fashionable scoop bonnet, Mrs. Adoniram Judson watched solemnly. As Dr. Griffin laid his hand on young Adoniram's head to pronounce his commission and benediction, he paused—remembering that this was the young man who had turned down his offer of a wealthy pulpit perhaps to starve, in India!

Less than two weeks later the trim little brig, the "Caravan," impatiently rocking at its moorings, received its load of freight and provisions, boarded its passengers, and then, sails glittering in the snowy winter air, moved out of Salem Bay. On deck the young Judsons and the young Newells watched the ragged New England coast grow dimmer and dimmer.

Such a honeymoon! The "Caravan's" cabins· were so pinched and narrow that you could hardly stand up straight and turn around in them. The decks slanted at such a rakish, dangerous angle most of the time that long walks were impractical. Yet Adoniram and Samuel insisted that everyone must have exercise. The problem was solved by laborious, studious rope-jumping on deck every sunny day. But a missionary could not spend all his time in frivolity—even as mild as jumping rope. He must study. And one problem in particular plagued Adoniram.

"I wish you'd never bothered your head about the Baptists." Ann shook her brown curls in honest distress.

"And get out there to India and work side by side with those Baptist powers, Carey and Ward and Marshman without sharpening up my arguments for my side? Nancy, you don't know what you're saying!"

"I know this: I don't like it. Maybe you've started

out sharpening up your Congregational arguments—but it sounds to me like you're more of a Baptist right this very minute."

"If I am, I didn't plan it that way. I wanted to be able to answer some native convert when he comes up to me and says—'Why you baptize my family, and Mr. Carey not?'"

"Maybe that's the way it started. But Don, darling, you've been arguing *against* yourself all this while."

Before he answered, Adoniram stared a long time at the even line of the horizon. "The way I figure it, Nancy, the *truth's* been arguing against me."

Ann was on her feet, wrapping her shawl around her thin shoulders. "You can go over to the other side, Adoniram Judson, and be a Baptist, but I'll tell you this: I'll be a Congregationalist as long as I live."

After they passed the Cape of Good Hope, the trip speeded along. On the seventeenth of June, about five months after they watched the New England coast disappear, the brig "Caravan" landed at Calcutta! The Judsons were in India!

At Calcutta Baptist missionary Carey welcomed them warmly. To him Adoniram confided his tussle with the matter of baptism. Carey suggested he wait for the rest of his party (they were coming from Philadelphia on the "Harmony") in Serampore, about ten miles up the river. While he was there, he could have access to many books, ample time to study!

Sweltering in the hot Indian sun, Ann and Adoniram spent the next three weeks studying. Yet Adoniram's mind was almost made up before he began the intensive reading. Even Ann was almost won over. And yet—!

The frightened look in her eyes when she talked about it must have twisted Adoniram's heart.

"I know, Nancy, I know. Will the Congregationalists support an immersing missionary? That's what you want to ask?"

"They won't. There isn't any need to ask." She was almost crying. "We'll be out here alone, without a cent or anyone to care!"

"But you do agree with me. It's the only thing to do."

Slowly Ann nodded. "To write to the American Board and tell them we've changed? Yes."

Reluctantly, Adoniram wrote the letters. First, one to the American Board of Foreign Commissioners. "The Board will, undoubtedly, feel as unwilling to support me as a missionary as I feel to comply with their instructions. I have now the prospect before me of going alone to some distant island."

He wrote a second one, addressed it to a Salem Baptist minister. "Should there be formed a Baptist society for the support of a mission in 'these parts, I should be ready to consider myself their missionary."

But before the letters reached the States, an unexpected blow fell. An official messenger arrived at Serampore and demanded the presence of Mr. Judson and Mr. Newell at the government house in Calcutta—immediately.

In Calcutta the swarthy, glowering police officer had nothing to say. He merely read a curt command from the governor-general. "The American missionaries must leave the country at once. When the 'Caravan' sails for the United States they must be on it!"

Chapter Five

THE LARGE AND HEAVY THUMB

A ND SO, MY DEAR YOUNG JUDSON, you have decided that it's wisest to obey the order from the British East India Company—and go home." William Carey, venerable, paunchy Baptist missionary, fanned himself vigorously in his Calcutta home and looked inquiringly at the two young missionaries.

"We have not!" Adoniram Judson exploded. "We crossed the ocean to preach the Gospel in the East, and the British East India has no right—"

"They have every right, or they think they do," the older missionary interrupted. "Let me explain. The British East India Company controls the commerce and, yes, most of the government, here in India. How does it maintain that control? By keeping a large and heavy thumb solidly on our dark-skinned natives! By telling them they are inferior! That they belong under that thumb! And what will Christianity teach them? That under Christ black men are equal with white! Do you see?"

Adoniram nodded furiously. "That way lies rebellion. That's how they figure, isn't it? They won't get away with it."

"Mr. Judson, you are a very young man, not yet twenty-five years old. Is that not right? Right now, no mission board supports or backs you. You don't even know the Indian language. It's laughable to think you could oppose the company."

"But that heavy thumb—it's not planted on *every* square inch of territory in the East?"

William Carey smiled wryly. "Not quite. They've missed a few islands. And Burma, now take Burma, a likely country for two young idealistic missionaries like yourself. Two Englishmen went out there to set up a mission not long ago. They abandoned it in quick order. A Portuguese priest, a native convert, was seized by the Burmese authorities, and beaten with an iron maul until he went insane. My own son, Felix, went to Burma and had to flee. When he married a native woman, he was allowed to return."

Ann shuddered, and Adoniram slipped his arm around her waist. "But these islands?"

"Haven't I convinced you yet? You've taken on a hopeless job."

"No! We're staying!"

William Carey fanned himself silently for a moment. "Excellent! That's what I wanted to hear. Now let me tell you about one of these islands, beyond the reach of the British East India—the Isle of France."

The Isle of France was a treacherous five thousand ocean-miles away, southeast near Madagascar. But to Adoniram and to the Newells, who determined to go with them, it seemed as if God Himself favored the decision to begin a mission there. A ship sailed that very week from Calcutta to the island's major city, Port Louis.

But there was one major drawback: only two passengers could squeeze aboard. Because fragile little Harriet Newell expected her first baby in a few months, the

couples agreed that ship's space belonged to the Newells. Adoniram and Ann would follow as soon as they
could.

That fall, spent with the Baptist missionaries at Serampore, was a nervous, restless time. Every shadow
that fell across the porch might be a British East India
official, come to deport Adoniram by force. The mails,
agonizingly slow, brought no word that the American
Baptists were even considering a financial stake in the
two young Judsons. The fall dragged on.

Shortly before the American Thanksgiving Day, the
British East India company chose a unique way to flex
its muscles and shake its fist in the Judsons' faces. As
they sat down to supper one night, someone rushed in
with a copy of the day's newspaper. As Adoniram opened
it, his own name leaped out at him from the passenger
list of the next London-bound ship! The heavy thumb
was crushing down; there could be no more stalling.

A frantic search of Calcutta docks revealed a single
boat bound for the Isle of France, and it would sail
before the deadline set for the Judsons' departure. Adoniram approached Calcutta's governor-general with a simple request, a passport for the ship, the "Creole." The
governor-general handed back a simple answer, an un-
equivocal "no." Obviously, he would offer the American
troublemakers no assistance in getting a foothold anywhere on the continent.

But Adoniram had another crafty and daring plan.
He approached the captain of the "Creole" himself.
Would he take two humble, harmless Americans aboard,
for a price, of course? The captain grinned and shrugged.

"It is my ship, Monsieur. Do as you please."

It was not quite as easy as that; the Judsons, with young Luther Rice, craftily plotted their escape from the mission station to the "Creole." If anyone detected their plans, they would be plucked up and dropped on board the London vessel! Waiting that night until the Calcutta streets were as black as ink and as deserted as the market-place on Buddha's birthday, Adoniram and Ann and young Rice sneaked stealthily out of the station, crept silently toward the docks, their luggage balanced precariously on servants' backs. Friendly natives swung open the gates to the docks. A few minutes later they were safely aboard, and the "Creole's" sails puffed out triumphantly as it slipped away from Calcutta.

After two days out the government dispatch overtook them. "You carry passengers expressly forbidden by the governor. Do not proceed until they are put ashore!"

Midstream in the Hoogli River, the "Creole" dropped anchor. The captain was sympathetic, but firm about the orders. And he had a schedule to keep, freight to deliver. He was so very sorry, but the missionaries must disembark.

A cramped little rowboat rocked them into shore, and they took shelter in a littered seaside tavern. At first they hoped to negotiate for a pass to continue. The captain of the "Creole" obligingly waited. But no pass came. As they watched and prayed, the captain fretted. Finally, he announced he must sail without them.

From the shore they watched the "Creole's" sails grow tinier. They were utterly abandoned. But the innkeeper tantalized them with a small hope. Another ship would put into this same port within days; he knew the captain. Maybe he could be reasoned with to take the missionaries aboard.

He couldn't. The innkeeper in great embarrassment confessed to Adoniram that the captain refused to traffic with outlawed American missionaries. Sitting down to supper that same night, the Judsons and Rice determined one last resort. What did they have to lose? They planned to see the captain themselves and argue their case.

At that very moment the governor's message arrived. They never knew whose influence had produced it, but they knew God's hand was there. The message said this: "Missionaries Ann Judson, Adoniram Judson and Luther Rice may proceed on the ship 'Creole.'"

But the "Creole" was gone, sailed some two or three days before! With good winds, a fast boat, and the right kind of tide, they might catch it at Saugur, down the river. But from Saugur the "Creole" would head straight out into the great wide bay; and any race with it then was laughable.

The only boat at hand was a leaky old rowboat; the tide swelled up and pushed them back. Furiously they rowed downstream, their baggage swaying in the clumsy tub. Could they reach Saugur in time? Or would they arrive to see the "Creole's" sails shimmering on the horizon? Their prayers must have kept rhythm with their rowing.

When they spotted the port of Saugur, they were afraid to look. Half a hundred ships stood at anchor in the Hoogli River where it joined the great bay—boats with tattered sails, weather-beaten hulls—flying flags from countries all over the world, waiting for cargoes. In the midst of them all was the "Creole!"

Almost a full year after they had sailed from Salem in January, 1813, Adoniram and Ann saw their destination, the Isle of France. But the mildness of that sunny January day and the loveliness of the island did not prepare them for the horror of the news they heard even before they landed. Blue sky reflected in the reef-bound harbor, filmy clouds brooded over the mountain summits, scarlet and blue blossoms tangled on the dark cliffs. And as they anchored in the bay, who climbed on deck but Sam Newell—exactly as they had anticipated.

Or was this lean man, with the gaunt cheeks and the dark-ringed eyes really Samuel Newell? Adoniram rushed to meet him with a great joyous leap and then stopped. Samuel walked toward him slowly, staring downward at the planks of the deck. In a moment both Adoniram and Ann guessed. Harriet, wistful, shy, thin little Harriet, was dead.

Samuel blurted out the whole pathetic story. The baby had been born at sea, had died in a few days. As Harriet weakened, the ship raced against time to rush her into port. Island doctors struggled, but it had been too late. Within a week she died. Hearing the story, Adoniram knew he could not stay on this deceptively tranquil island, nor could he ask Ann to. But if they didn't settle on the Isle of France, where could they go next?

They decided on the Prince of Wales Island; the British East India Company could not hound them there. But to reach Prince of Wales, they must touch briefly at Madras within the company's jurisdiction. They would risk it.

In June Adoniram and Ann landed in Madras, entirely alone. Luther Rice had sailed to America to stir up lagging missionary interest among Baptists; Sam Newell had sailed to Bombay.

If Adoniram, embarking quietly in Madras, hoped to mingle with the natives on the streets without attracting attention, he found out quickly how foolishly optimistic he had been. Such information had a strange way of leaking into the governor-general's office. The British East India company, like a bulldog with a rat, shook its mighty head again. The American missionaries must leave the city immediately. Just to make certain, the company imposed a rigid deadline; they must be out within two weeks.

A frantic combing of the docks turned up one dismaying fact: boats sailed to Prince of Wales Island only on schedule. Not one was scheduled before the company's deadline!

But Adoniram and Ann had promised God; they would not go back on their word. He would sail on any boat at all, going anywhere, unless it were headed for England or the States. Wherever he was taken, he would begin his mission.

One flimsy old vessel leaned wearily at anchor, its mast crazily askew. Adoniram approached a swarthy-skinned, turbanned dockhand. Yes, the sailing date for this miserable tub came up before the deadline.

"Where to?" Adoniram asked. The dockhand grinned, a three-toothed evil grin.

"Burma, sahib!"

Burma! He might have said the country where the only Christian mission stood abandoned and rotting, the country where they beat Christian converts until they went insane! Burma! He might as well have said "Gehenna."

Chapter Six

THE CAPITAL SWAMP

I<small>T'S FILTHIER AND HOTTER</small> and meaner than anybody told us—even Carey!" Inside the cabin, a mere flimsy canvas shelter propped up on the deck of the crazy old vessel "Georgiana," the slender young American missionary sat, head in hands, beside his wife who lay, too sick to sit up, on a narrow cot. "It's nothing but a sludgy, squdgy swamp!"

"But Don—Rangoon, isn't it one of the capital cities?" Ann spoke weakly.

"A capital swamp. That's what it is! A city of tumble-down bamboo shacks on stilts. And Ann—" Adoniram shuddered, "the pigs live under the houses and eat the garbage. The dogs look wild, like they'd run in out of the jungle to feed on all the refuse lying in the street. And, oh, Ann—" Adoniram's sensitive nose lifted, "the smell!"

Ann turned her face toward the canvas wall.

"They put their dovecotes up on poles, and I found out why. To protect the doves from wildcats! That's your capital city of Rangoon. That's our mission field!" Adoniram spoke bitterly.

"Doesn't sound much like Boston," Ann looked as if she were trying to smile.

"And Burma isn't like our United States. The government's insane, Ann—a cruel, treacherous dictatorship, that's all. The country's cut up into provinces, and each one is ruled over by a gentleman who calls himself an Eater!"

"An Eater!" Ann giggled.

"That's no laughing matter. From what I can figure out, that's exactly what he does: gobbles up as much as he can grab from the peasants for himself and his underlings, and I almost forgot, the Lord of the White Elephant," Adoniram finished sarcastically.

"You mean—the king?"

"The Golden Nose himself. Everything about him is gold. At least his subjects think so or have to think so!" he broke off. "Six weeks on this crazy old tub, you losing the baby and almost dying, and where do we land? In the rubbish dump of the Orient!"

The next day—it was July 13, 1813—they disembarked. Ann, still too miserable to walk, was carried ashore by obliging Burmese, toted through the main streets of town while curious natives stared at the first white woman ever to come to Rangoon. Adoniram trotted beside the makeshift portable chair, uneasily aware of the wide-eyed, giggling women.

They were two lonely youngsters, not yet twenty-five years old, who after traveling for more than a year and a half without finding a stopping place, came to this country completely uninvited, without even knowing a word of the language. And they came to do a stupendous task—to convert people who never before had even heard the name of Jesus Christ! They had no political pull, no influential friends, no plan to win over the high places first; they were simply ready to fight with old-fashioned truths. They planned to meet Buddhism that declared there was no god to save, no soul to be saved, and no sin to be saved from, with the Christian truth that God was real, man was sinful, and that Christ had died on the cross to save anyone who would believe.

As young Adoniram stood in the burning heat of that Burmese July day, staring back at the great golden Shwe Dagon Pagoda that overshadowed the entire city, he did not guess the terribleness of the discouragement that waited for him in the muddy streets of Rangoon —that he would work fifteen hours a day for six full years before he would win a single convert; four years would pass before anyone would even stop to ask about this strange Christianity; that the dismal stench, the rotten air of the tropic would break Ann's health. He would know physical pain as he never had known it. His second child would die (the first had been born dead on the "Georgiana"). And in all the six years most Andover graduates of his class were building up tidy little New England congregations and rearing their families in cool, healthy New England air.

But to Adoniram, settling into Felix Carey's house that July, his job seemed very simple and clear cut. Logically, he and Ann must first master the language.

But the Burmese language was as tangled as a "bad knitter's skein of wool," Ann said. Words stretched on and on endlessly, and then turned out to be whole sentences or paragraphs. No periods or commas broke in for readability. Bundles of old palm leaves were the only books; words were scratched on the leaves in a haphazard sort of way. No one had ever written a

Burmese dictionary, and who would ever have need of a grammar!

"A dead language, like Latin, is hard enough to learn," Adoniram wrote home in discouragement. "But have you ever tried to master a living one where the idioms change almost every day and nobody bothers to record them?"

To find a teacher who knew both English and Burmese was absolutely impossible. Nobody in all Rangoon spoke English, not even Felix Carey's wife, for she was a Burman, and Felix was away on a government junket. Adoniram prepared himself to learn from an intelligent Burman the hardest way of all—pointing and grunting.

But he was not at all prepared for the teacher's violent sputtering at the start of the first lesson. The teacher had come to teach one student—a man! Teach a woman to write and read? Might as well waste your time trying to train a monkey from the jungle! Only more money convinced him to take over the futile, disagreeable task.

Study began at seven in the morning, in the cool of the day, endured the heat of noon, and did not end until the moon had risen over the great Shwe Dagon Pagoda. Sitting cross-legged on the veranda floor with the teacher, grunting, pointing, Adoniram studied. Inside the house at her own table, Ann worked along with the lesson, directing the marketing, the cooking, the housework with half her mind and energies. (By now they had settled into their own mission house within the city walls.) Chances are she learned more Burmese from her conversation with the market boys than she learned from her respectable, scholarly teacher.

Painstakingly, they learned to wrap their tongues around the ungiving Burmese words. But a full year after they had landed, in July, 1814, they were still studying. "I knew more about French in two months than I know about Burmese now," Adoniram agonized in a letter home. Preach? Convert anyone? They could hardly order their groceries in this complicated, grammarless, mass of strange syllables.

In January, 1815, they were still plodding along when Ann's health broke.

Drugs that would have helped were undiscovered; native doctors were only baffled by the white woman's queer reaction to normal Burmese weather. There was only one cure for what the tropic weather was doing to her—she must escape from it. A sea voyage was the solution, and so Ann left the mission house and Adoniram for three full months. When she returned in March, Adoniram still struggled with the words.

For a few brief months, life seemed easier. In September, 1814, they heard the good news of their appointment as Baptist missionaries. Later that month, little Roger Williams Judson was born, a healthy boy who cried a lot, laughed even more, and then gradually, as his parents watched helplessly, lost the strength to laugh or cry. The Burmese climate slowly destroyed him. When Roger was only eight months old, he died. They buried him in a little grove of mango trees in the mission garden.

When the headaches began, a month after his son's death, Adoniram wouldn't admit their existence. Was it Ann who noticed his twitching, reddened eyes? Staring at the scratches on the dried palm leaves for fifteen hours a day had damaged his eyes badly. They burned, itched constantly. His head throbbed as if a burning pike were driven through half his skull; with every throb a strong giant drove the pike deeper. Lying in bed for a month in a dark room, Adoniram wondered if God had stopped him even before he finished laying the foundation, before he started to build.

Did his stubbornness get the better of Ann's solicitous nursing? Even in his darkened room he recklessly dug away at his study. On July 13, 1816, exactly three years to the very day after he landed in Rangoon, he finished the first step of his missionary work—his Burmese-English grammar.

Now he could spell out salvation in words any Burman could understand. That month he wrote his first tract.

In October of that same year he delightedly welcomed into Rangoon a man who would make that one tract preach to thousands—George Hough, a printer by trade. American Baptists sent Hough to Burma. Luther Rice had been busy back in the States, indeed. The Baptists banded together to stand behind this missionary, Judson, who so amazingly thrust himself into their midst. They were going to support him financially, and in any tangible way possible. British Baptists donated a printing press and a complete font of Burmese type.

Adoniram helped the homespun, kindly Hough set up shop in the bamboo mission house. Soon a thousand copies of his Burmese tract rolled off his press. Three thousand of Ann's own catechism were printed next.

For four years his studies, his preparation were slow

and laborious. Then in March, 1817, with the suddenness of a lizard sliding off the bamboo roof onto the dinner table, the first Burmese inquirer mounted the mission porch. Followed by his servant, the well-gowned middle-aged Burman walked up and asked a direct question.

"How long time will it take me to learn the religion of Jesus?"

Adoniram looked at him steadily. "Without God, you can study all your life and still not learn. What brought you here? How did you come to know anything at all of Jesus, even His name? Have you been here before?"

"No."

"Have you seen any writings about Jesus?"

"I have seen two little books."

"Then you tell me—who is Jesus?"

"He is the Son of God, who, pitying creatures, came into this world and suffered death in their stead." He spoke mechanically as if he had recently memorized this fact.

"Then who is God?"

"He is a Being without beginning or end, who is not subject to old age and death but always is." The man still spoke mechanically.

Feeling as if he might be dreaming, Adoniram held out a copy of his tract. The Burman took it, nodded. "I read this. Do you not have something more?"

"Only part of a book. It's not finished. Come back in maybe three months, it'll be done."

"But have you not a little of book done, which you can graciously give me now?" the Burman persisted.

Reluctantly, yet sure that God's time was wiser than his, Adoniram handed over what he had completed of his translation of the Bible into Burmese—the first five chapters of Matthew. The Burman nodded formally, smiled slightly and left.

Adoniram now rushed through his translation of Matthew. Two days after he had finished, he began another job—a Burmese-English dictionary! He could speak, write, and read the language. People were obviously reading his tracts. Preaching services must begin immediately!

But he didn't *think* Burmese. He needed an assistant who did, one to check any embarrassing mistakes. In Chittagong a tiny seacoast strip, Baptist missionaries had worked for years; the converts spoke Burmese and English too. Adoniram determined to sail to Chittagong to persuade a convert to come back as his assistant, then he could start his missionary work in earnest!

"Seems like God's will, Ann," he told his wife that December night, 1817. "The ship is sailing straight from Rangoon to Chittagong and returning. God must have planned it. This way the trip'll take me only three months."

"Three months'll seem like three years."

"But Ann—"

"And I have enough to do in those three months to keep me busy for three years. Go ahead. Get us a nice assistant—and Don, do hurry back!"

Ann's mind and hands were full that winter—her house, her language study, her catechisms. But toward the end of March she began to watch the muddy Irrawaddy River for the first hazy line of the returning ship. Finally there was one vessel, and it had sailed from Chittagong twelve days before.

But Adoniram did not stride down the gangplank. She waited forlornly on the dock until the ship's captain crossed over to her. He eyed her sadly. "I hate to be the one to tell you, ma'am, but that ship that Mr. Judson was on—" he looked down at the dock, "well, ma'am, it never did reach Chittagong at all. Nobody's heard a word about it!"

Chapter Seven

MOSLEMS, MERCHANTS, AND DIRTY BEGGARS

TO A MAN WHO KNEW so precisely where he was
going when he started out, the trick that the ocean
winds played on Adoniram's ship was a cruel one! The
ship headed straight toward Chittagong but almost before it had nosed out of Rangoon Bay, violent winds
battered and buffeted it about. For weeks the ship
zigzagged, until the captain made a desperate decision
to change his course radically and sail, not toward the
coast of Burma, but across the Bay of Bengal to Madras
in India instead. That India was the last place in the
world one of his passengers wanted to go made no
difference.

As the ship muddled into the great wide Bay of
Bengal, Adoniram watched the Burmese mountains sink
lower and lower. With them his dream of hiring an
English-speaking assistant sank, too.

He soothed his impatience with the bright thought
that ships often sailed from Madras to Rangoon; he could
at least, return by March as he planned. But close to
Madras the wind shifted suddenly and the captain
declared that landing was an impossibility. Instead, he
would head for an obscure little port to the north,
Masulipatam.

But food and water supply ran perilously low. Sometimes a sister ship passed close enough to the foundering little ship to toss on board a bucket of water or a bag of rice. The old eye trouble came back to torment Adoniram with its stabbing misery. He lay in bed, eating only an occasional handful of dirty rice, moaning for water when he had the strength, worrying in a half-delirium about Ann. He already was a month overdue in Rangoon!

In May the ship limped dispiritedly into the forsaken port of Masulipatam, on north India's shore. Disembarking, Adoniram inquired for the quickest ship to Madras. From Madras, he could book passage to Rangoon. But no ships had sailed from Masulipatam to Madras all year. None were likely to sail for months. There he was—thousands of miles from home, unable to communicate with Ann, no way of reaching a boat to Rangoon and fretting about what was happening to her.

Had he known, he would have worried more intensely. Cholera dotted the filthy streets of Rangoon. The death gong boomed every day. In almost every bamboo shack somebody died. Whispers of war between Burma and England shadowed the atmosphere. At the mission the Houghs got panicky.

"Every British ship's left the harbor but one. If you want to get out of this confounded city alive, Mrs. Judson, you better hop onto that one with us."

Ann was unconvinced. In this whole Asiatic continent, Rangoon was the only place that Adoniram could find her.

"But you don't even know, Mrs. Judson, if—if he's coming back."

With New England bluntness, the Houghs faced the

unpleasant facts. They begged Ann to value her own
life. So she gave in, allowing the Houghs to carry her
baggage shipboard, saying good-bye to her teacher and
her servants. The last British ship rolled sickeningly out
of Rangoon Harbor and down the muddy Irrawaddy.

Where the Irrawaddy joins the open bay, the ship
dropped anchor. The captain apologized profusely for
the unplanned, unscheduled delay. In spite of his careful
supervision, the ship was overloaded to the point of
being tipsily unseaworthy. If the passengers would be
patient, the error would be corrected in short order.

"Get my baggage!" Ann declared. She made up her
mind. She was returning to Rangoon. There she would
wait for Adoniram her whole life if she had to.

Shortly after she unlocked the Rangoon mission house,
almost before she greeted all her servants, Adoniram returned! With all sea routes to Madras blocked, he had
traveled to the port by land, hiring a palanquin and
bearers to carry him more than three hundred miles
over rough jungle terrain. In Madras he had found a
ship sailing to Rangoon.

He was gone more than seven months on a trip that
should have taken three; he returned without accom-
plishing one small fraction of the job he set out for.
But he was home in Rangoon with Ann, alive and well!

"And I'm not waiting one day more to preach the
Gospel," he vowed. "I'm taking it to the people—their
way. I'm going to build myself a schoolhouse, but not
the New England variety. It'll be Burmese style!"

Ann's eyes widened. "A *zayat?* Don, you wouldn't
dare!"

Did Adoniram think of the New England village greens

framed by white-spired churches as he leased his hand-
kerchief plot of land along the hot city highway? When
he measured the space, just twenty-seven feet by eighteen, slapped on the whitewash and twisted the bamboo
and thatch into place, did he wistfully recall "the biggest
church in Boston?" Or did he only remember the six
long years spent in tedious, time-marking study, exuber-
ant at last that he had some place, any place to preach
God's Word!

The *zayat* was as Burmese as betel juice, exactly
like any other Rangoon schoolhouse. In front along the
highway was an open veranda, sheltered by a bamboo
roof. On this veranda Adoniram took up his post every
morning, sitting cross-legged on the floor, his stentorian
voice accosting every man or woman with Scripture
as they walked down the highway. "Ho, everyone that
thirsteth!"

Inside, in the second and third rooms, Ann taught
her school. The men sat meekly in rows in front of her
in the second room. In the third room, the women,
chastely separate, studied the same lesson.

At first Adoniram worried about his audience. Would
anyone draw off the highway to hear him read about
the new religion? He didn't worry long. Women, their
eyelids and teeth blackened with betel juice, winked
and grinned at the white man. But they stopped on their
way to market to hear him read a chapter or two. Mos-
lems in brilliant turbans stood and stared up at him,
flashing blasé, arrogant eyes. Wealthy merchants ordered their servants to shelter them from the sun with
wide umbrellas as they listened to the missionary. Even
dirty beggars limped up to the veranda to rest and

hear the truth. After his first *zayat* service on April 4,
1819, Adoniram never worried about an audience.

But whether anyone in all this disorderly, restless
crowd listened, neither Adoniram nor Ann were quite
sure—not sure, that is, until the *zayat* drew its crowd
for a month. Then in the first week of May they won
their very first convert to Christianity. They had been
in Burma almost six years!

Their first convert was a simple fellow, hired by a
lumber merchant to do general labor. He had no family,
no money, no education. But Moung Nau was sincerely
converted.

"It seems almost too much to believe that God has
begun to manifest His grace to the Burmans," Adoniram
scribbled joyously in his diary that night. "Praise and
glory be to His name forevermore!" On June 27, 1819,
he baptized Moung Nau.

Adoniram preached with fiercer zest. Another Burman
accepted Christ—Moung Tha Hla, an intelligent, well-
educated fellow. Then a third convert, Moung Bya,
declared his disillusionment with Buddhism, his belief in
Christianity. A learned Rangoon schoolteacher stopped
often to question. Several women, smiling impersonally
under the flower blossoms in their hair, nodded gravely
when Adoniram asked them if they would accept Christ
as their Saviour. To him it was very clear; God had
begun to work in the hearts of Burmans.

He found out all too quickly that Satan was not idle!
Some malicious tattletale whispered to Rangoon's viceroy that many citizens were finding spiritual satisfaction in the white man's *zayat*. Even a well-known schoolteacher was observed to enter. "Inquire further about

that one!" the viceroy roared. The sad news crept quickly through Rangoon's streets. Any Burman who declared the American religion right and the Buddhist way wrong would be severely punished.

The curious and the almost-persuaded shied away from the little *zayat*. They knew the viceroy defined "severe" with an iron maul or a lashing whip.

Even Adoniram dared not baptize the faithful openly. He led Moung Hla and Moung Bya to a solitary pool on the outskirts of town. In the gloom of sunset he baptized them. With this feeble, solitary little band of believers, he asked God's forgiveness for his timidity.

Soon after, as he rode to the mineral tank for his daily bath, a ranking Buddhist churchman halted his carriage. Glowering at him, threatening him with a beating, the churchman shouted, "Stop your preaching, American missionary, or be very, very sorry."

The whole town trembled. It looked as if the blackjack of persecution would beat the life right out of the tiny Burman "church" before it started to breathe.

With the courage and the cunning of a Burman tiger, Adoniram decided on a plan that could either ruin his entire missionary venture or vindicate him once and for all over the Rangoon viceroy. He decided to pay a most courteous call to the Golden One himself, the king of all Burma, and ask his honorable permission not only to preach the heretical religion, but to translate the Bible into the language of the land!

And what, actually, did he have to lose? If the Golden Head nodded permission, Christianity was safe in the country. If he refused, Adoniram was only where he was before he asked.

Leaving Ann in Rangoon, Adoniram sailed up the Irrawaddy, taking with him young James Coleman, new addition to the Rangoon missionary staff. Cutting into the Burmese interior, the Irrawaddy was hot and slimy. Adoniram's ship was no wider than a man is tall, just six feet, and only forty feet long. In the stern thin boards built up the sides slightly, across them lay a thatch roof. In this "cabin," Adoniram and Coleman could barely lie or sit down. They journeyed in it for more than a month.

From the docks in Ava, Adoniram and young Coleman labored on foot for miles along a dirty road underneath the broiling sun. The road, for all its dustiness, led directly to the golden gate of the royal palace!

But at the gate a guard detained them impersonally. If their pass proved to be in order, they might at least be permitted to see the minister of state.

At last they were ushered into the wide, glittering palace yard. The minister of state greeted them, chatted casually, but the Golden One was nowhere to be seen.

"So sorry!" the minister of state apologized. "Someone should have told the Americans. This is not a good day. It is a special ceremonial day!"

In quiet despair Adoniram handed over his petition for religious tolerance. He explained that they were "missionaries, propagators of religion, if he preferred."

A remote rustle from the inner palace! Handing back the petition hastily, the minister fumbled into his robe. Someone announced that the Golden Foot approached. Nervously, Adoniram clutched the gold-leaf Bible, his present for the king. The rustle of a silken gown drew closer, and the minister of state turned to Adoniram with a shrug.

"How can you propagate religion in this empire? But come along! I will introduce you!"

Chapter Eight

"THERE IS ONE BEING"

WHEN THE YOUNG KING strode imperiously into the great gold-domed hall, only two foreheads did not respectfully burrow into the dust—the foreheads of Adoniram Judson and young James Coleman. The American missionaries in their long white surplice gowns stared steadily back at the youthful eastern monarch, their knees lightly touching the ground, their hands folded.

"Who are these?" The great Golden One brandished his gold-sheathed sword like a sceptre.

Adoniram's throat felt raw and dry. "The teachers, great king!"

"What! You speak Burmese!" The king's foot moved as if it would nudge the missionary, then withdrew cautiously. "When did you come? You are teachers of religion? Are you like the Portuguese priest? Are you married? Why do you dress so?"

The majestic youth listened gravely as Adoniram answered. Wrapping his brocaded robe about him grandly, he mounted the throne. Crawling forward in the dust, the minister of state lifted Adoniram's petition and read it in a high, querulous voice.

"The American teachers present themselves to receive the favor of the excellent king, the sovereign of land and sea . . . and ask . . . that royal permission be given, that we, taking refuge in the royal power, may preach our religion in these dominions, and that those who are pleased with our preaching, and wish to listen to and be guided by it, whether foreigners or Burman, may be exempt from government molestations."

Wordlessly the monarch stretched out his hand. The minister of state, inching toward him on the ground, laid the parchment on the great Golden Hand. On top of the petition he placed Adoniram's tract.

"There is one Being who exists eternally . . . and beside Him, there is no other God . . . " With an insolence as brittle as his sword's gold sheath, the king and sovereign of all Burma flung the tract to the dust. He read no more than the first sentence. Pages of the petition scattered like so many palm leaves on the ground. Nervously unfolding one of the gold-leaf volumes, the minister of state held it up, as if he would tempt this irritable young man. But the interview was irrevocably over.

"In regard to the objects of your petition, his majesty gives no order! In regard to your sacred books, his majesty has no use for them. Take them away!"

There was no sense in telling a pleasant myth back in Rangoon. On the hot, tedious boat-journey down the Irrawaddy, Adoniram accepted the truth. The emperor had refused permission to preach Christ to any living soul under his thumb. Any Burman who renounced Buddhism stood in line for jail—or death.

In Rangoon Adoniram hailed his three faithful converts and broke an incredible piece of news to them. He was abandoning his mission. He would lock the *zayat*. They could do with it as they wanted. He was going to sail for Chittagong. There he could preach in Burmese but he would be safe, blessed by the protection of the British flag.

Nothing in all his discouraging years prepared him for the astounding reaction of the three Burmese converts!

"I will go with you," said Moung Nau.

"I cannot," said another, "because of my wife and children. But I will be faithful to the death here—even if you desert us."

"But don't abandon us," they all pleaded. "Now is the time for teaching. Interested ones come to our door every day. We alone do not know enough to teach them the great truths."

"If I stay, look, you know what persecution means in this crazy government."

"Stay until a little church of ten is collected, and you have placed a native teacher over it. Then go, if you must. If there are ten of us, the religion will spread of itself. The superiors cannot stop it. No, not even with persecution."

Adoniram could not argue down such faith. He and Ann stopped inquiring about passage to Chittagong. They decided to stay in Rangoon. They remembered their old prayer, "God grant that we may live and die among the Burmans, though we never should do anything else than smooth the way for others!"

Like the roots of the trees along the banks of the Irrawaddy, the little Burmese church flourished—underground. That the great Golden Hand doubled into a fist and shook in their very faces made no difference to the curious and the converted. The learned skeptic schoolteacher, who had teetered so long, said flatly he was a Christian, even if he died for it. More women came to worship in the *zayat*. By the middle of 1820 the tenth convert bowed his head and acknowledged his Saviour.

But hard on the heels of this astounding triumph came discouragement. Ann was desperately sick, and she could never be cured anywhere in the East. The East, with its steaming heat and its uncontrolled germs, could be blamed for her fevers and dysentery. She must get out as fast as the next boat could take her.

When Adoniram put her on board the British vessel, he knew that two full years must pass before he would see her again. From his diary he made no attempt to camouflage his loneliness. "If we could find some quiet resting place on earth where we might spend the rest of our days together in peace!"

Yet he did not forget to steady himself with this remarkable postscript, "Life is short. Millions of Burmans are perishing. I am almost the only person on earth who has attained their language to communicate salvation."

Here it was—the reason that Adoniram fought against fever, persecution, loneliness. The reason he stuck with the church in Rangoon. The reason that sent him up the dirty Irrawaddy a second time to ask the king's permission to evangelize Burma!

Shortly after Ann left for the States, two new missionaries joined the Rangoon station, Dr. Jonathan Price and his wife. Young Mrs. Price died five months after she landed; they buried her beside little Roger Williams Judson.

But young Jonathan stuck it out. With his skilled,

sure knife, he gained quick fame throughout the city. Especially remarkable was his success with cataracts. News of his uncanny ability to give a man new eyes even reached Ava. And the Golden Eyes himself commanded his presence, immediately!

Price knew little Burmese. Naturally, for the Ava excursion he needed an interpreter. There was no more logical person for that job than Adoniram. They left Rangoon in August, 1822, saying good-bye wistfully to a Rangoon church that now numbered eighteen converts!

If Adoniram trembled because the king might recognize him immediately and order him banished or imprisoned, he wasted his worry. The king was far too intrigued with the bag of magic in the doctor's possession. Could he, would he, prolong the royal life for many years? The Golden One never looked twice at the interpreter-missionary, so dull in his sedate black suit.

The daily interviews were almost over when the king raised a questioning eyebrow. "You in black, what are you? A medical man?"

"Not a medical man, but a teacher of religion, your majesty."

"Religion, eh?" The king fingered his robe. "And have any embraced this—uh—religion of yours?"

"Not here," Adoniram evaded.

"Are there any in Rangoon, then?"

Not even a fly buzzed in the vast hall. "There are a few."

"Are they foreigners?"

The truth might crush the little Rangoon church.

"There are some foreigners and—" he spoke quickly from a dry throat, "and some Burmans."

The king was silent. Adoniram waited. "God, bless Burma today," he prayed. But nothing happened. And, after a few perfunctory questions about geometry and astronomy, the king retired.

Soon after, his majesty royally beckoned to young Dr. Price to join the court staff. Price agreed to stay in Ava. In a sudden burst of good nature over capturing this prize, the monarch asked Adoniram to stay too. He granted him permission to buy a plot of ground so that he might build a suitable place to live—and a place to teach religion!

The incredible had happened. Shaking with chills one day, burning with fever the next, but praising God constantly, Adoniram sailed down the Irrawaddy to Rangoon. He planned to meet Ann there and return to the capital immediately.

When he arrived in Rangoon, a letter from Ann announced the discouraging news that she had sailed from England to America. She would not be back for almost a year. The Rangoon mission would have to wait.

Yet one important job needed a long breathing space granted by this delay. Adoniram still dreamed of the day when he could put a complete Bible into the hands of any literate Burman. During the next ten months before Ann's arrival, he sweated through the entire New Testament, had completed it, and in December had written a hasty resumé of the Old Testament.

With his usual brusque directness, he ordered Ann's baggage taken immediately from the ship on which she had arrived and loaded on a small craft to sail up the

Irrawaddy. Eight days later Adoniram and Ann left the mission in Rangoon under the supervision of four other American missionaries. They were about to begin what they had every right to expect was their most successful work, right under the nose of the Burmese king.

The trip along the wide, slow-moving river was pleasant and leisurely. Adoniram and Ann had not been together for two and a half years; there was so much to talk about. Occasionally, they left the boat, exploring the little villages on the banks, walking fast enough in the hot sun to catch up again along the route. There was nothing at all in the journey to foreshadow the dismal news that met them just before they sailed into the port of Ava.

Jonathan Price met them somewhat downstream in his small craft. His bad news was this: since Adoniram had left Ava ten months before, the entire privy council, from minister of state right down to the most lowly clerk, had been tossed out by a whim of the king. The council who favored Adoniram were as powerless now as the dogs that ran wild in the streets. And this new privy council did not like foreigners—teachers, missionaries, or doctors!

Yet Adoniram determined to go ahead exactly as if these rumors had never reached him. Ann invited young women to learn reading and writing at her school. At Price's quarters Adoniram preached every Sunday. Slowly, the work took hold.

It was a matter of high state coupled by a freakish instance of Burmese ignorance that smashed all of Adoniram's plans! One Sunday when the Judsons were at Dr. Price's home, and Adoniram had just finished his morning prayers, a messenger darted into the house with startling news. The British Army had invaded Burma! Rangoon had been bombarded and captured. A full-scale war was on!

Actually, the war had threatened for years. For years refugees from the tyranny of the Burmese king found sanctuary in Chittagong, under British rule. Burmese government had issued time and again an ultimatum ordering that the British return these refugees. If they did not, Burma would seize Chittagong.

When the British saw the Burmans meant business, they beat them to the draw. General Archibald Campbell, at the head of an army of five thousand, crossed the Irrawaddy and marched on Rangoon.

With Rangoon in British hands, Ava was in a panic. Pagoda gongs sounded mournfully all day long. But the Burmese were naively hopeful. They dispatched their own armies, generals astride mountainous elephants, gloating over the future British downfall, and, in the rear young boys dancing gleefully off to be killed. One general's high-caste wife gave her order for "four trustworthy white servants."

The Burmese never doubted their ultimate victory, but they were, nevertheless, furious that they had been so humiliated in Rangoon. It would not have happened if secrets had not leaked out from within.

And what more logical source of secrets than a white-skinned foreigner in the capital itself!

And here was conclusive proof: this white man, Moung Judson, had been seen getting money from a British bank. With a total lack of comprehension of a checking account, the Burmese reasoned he must be in the employ of the British government to receive money from them!

One night as Adoniram and Ann sat down to supper, an Ava police officer pushed open their door.

"Moung Judson," he snarled. "You are summoned to the king." Even the Americans knew the meaning of this Burmese idiom. It meant simply this: "You are under arrest."

Chapter Nine

HAND-SHRINK-NOT

THE POLICE OFFICER and his rabble company thrust into the house. In their midst Adoniram spied a man with a spotted face! He knew this old Burmese custom—any man with a spotted face was an executioner!

The spotted man seized Adoniram's arm, pitching him to the floor as if he were so much bamboo kindling. As Adoniram went down, he saw Ann pull frantically at the executioner's arm. "Stop," she cried, "I'll give you money!"

The burly executioner shrugged her off. "Take her," he said. "She also is a foreigner."

"Kill me! Burn the whole house! But don't touch Ann," Adoniram begged.

Now the whole street was in confusion. The bricklayers next door laid down their tools and tumbled after each other down the street. Little Burmese children screamed for their mothers. The Bengalese servants stood by open-mouthed.

The executioner went grimly to work, winding a thick rope around Adoniram's shoulders, yanking it tighter and tighter until he choked and gasped for breath. Ann shook money in the face of the spotted one, but with a growl, he shoved Adoniram toward the door.

On June 8, 1824, Adoniram was clapped into jail for

a crime he never committed. And if his fastidious senses cringed at the French prison—what did he think when he stood in the doorway of the Let-Ma-Yoon, death prison for all of Ava!

They had named it well; Let-Ma-Yoon means Hand-Shrink-Not! Every nerve shrank from the frightful smell of the squalid place. Rumor said it had not been washed or even swept since it had been built. Adoniram believed it. The floor was matted with rotting animals, human filth, the infernal betel juice spit from the drooling mouths of a thousand or more prisoners. Only chinks in the bamboo roof ventilated the wretched shed; there were no windows, and the jailer kept the bamboo door tightly closed. Under the Burmese sun the temperature shot up to 100 almost every day!

More than a hundred prisoners, men and women, jammed into this hut. Stocks clutched the feet and hands of some. Fetters knifed into the flesh of others. Some were strung up on bamboo poles like so much meat in the market-place.

Five fetters clamped down on Adoniram's legs, and he bore the scars until the day he died. Two iron rings, one around each ankle, were joined by a chain so short he could hardly drag the heel of one foot up to the toe of the other. When he walked, he shuffled a few short inches at a time.

The first night was terrible. Adoniram—the man who demanded fresh linen every day, who dusted his own orderly piles of papers and books, who insisted on a fresh black ribbon tie, even if it went limp from over-washing—lay down in the matted, odiferous filth in a long line of half-naked, sweating, stinking prisoners.

Through the chains on his feet the jailer slid a bamboo pole, raising it with fiendish precision until only Adoniram's shoulders rested on the ground. This way he slept, the circulation cut off enough to numb, not quite enough to kill!

But even on the softest cot, he wouldn't have slept. What had happened to Ann? She was the only white English-speaking woman in a city insanely incensed against foreign traitors!

Ann, of course, kept her head. She found herself placed immediately under twenty-four hour military guard. But when a magistrate arrived to confiscate her goods, she treated him with such adroitness she was permitted to keep Adoniram's books, her supply of medicine, and her work table. Minutes before the authorities arrived to comb the house, she rushed out to the garden with Adoniram's most precious possession—his still unfinished manuscript of the Burmese Bible. He had worked on this for ten years, and there was only one copy anywhere in the world! It must not—even if she suffered jail for it herself—be lost!

A few days after his capture, as Adoniram lay sweating in the hot box, Gouger, a young British merchant, inched over. "Your wife's here," he whispered.

He might have known! Ann with her winsomeness had talked her way right into the jail. Even as he crawled over to the doorway, dragging his fetters and chains over the rough floor, she stood wooing the jailer with her smiles and gentle talk. Aware that he hadn't shaved for days, that he was alive with small vermin, that he smelled as evilly as the dirtiest ruffians, Adoniram wasn't quite ready for Ann's look of horror as she covered her face with her hands and began to sob!

That very day Ann began her round of desperate attempts to speed Adoniram's release. In the next six months she daily begged someone to give the innocent Americans freedom.

She visited or wrote letters to every influential person she had ever known in Ava. Especially did she concentrate on the fat, jovial old governor, calling on him in person day after day! The governor listened, he was sympathetic, but he had no power to grant release. He did promise one thing: to stay Adoniram's execution!

This promise was small comfort to Adoniram. At night he and Gouger and young Dr. Price, captured too, heard the guards sharpening up their knifes for to-morrow's beheading. They heard wild rumors that someone would hold a torch to the bamboo shed, and they and the filth would go up in flames together. A captured lion roared in the little prison yard; this was immediate grounds for speculation. Would they be tossed out as food to the starving creature?

Adoniram fretted about his Burmese Bible too. He knew that Ann had buried it, but he imagined worms and mold eating through the precious syllables. Would ten years of constant study disappear in the damp ground of a Burmese garden?

One day Ann smuggled into him a pillow. The jailer gave her permission to bring food, and, if she smiled brightly enough, something as innocent as a pillow for the prisoner's comfort.

But this one was so lumpy! Adoniram felt it, looked

up querulously. "Ann, darling, couldn't you find a softer—"

But Ann shook her head, a mysterious gleam in her eyes. In a low whisper she told the astounding tale. She had dug up his precious manuscript and camouflaged it into a pillow. Who would suspect its presence, and who would covet a pillow so lumpy? Now he could sleep on his Bible every night, comforted by its nearness!

Trapped in the stinking prison, with no hope of release until the British whipped the Burmese, watching one prisoner a day led out for execution, Adoniram suffered six long and miserable months. A woman was brought into the prison covered with smallpox. Fortunately, no one caught the disease; the guard removed her the next day.

There were petty little annoyances too. Young Price, troubled with nightmares, poked his knees violently into Adoniram's back. Those nights he slept miserably, lashing out at young Price in uncontrollable irritation.

Ann's heroic chase from governor to magistrate harassed him. But her small kindnesses made his misery even more intense. One day Moung Ing, faithful convert, carried a mysterious-looking parcel into the jail. It was from Ann, and Adoniram ripped open the wrapping eagerly. There was an old-fashioned New England mince pie, contrived of buffalo meat and plantains! He could stand the jailer's curses, but not this pathetic attempt, this womanly tenderness of his brave wife! Stifling his tears, he shuffled away to be alone. Some other lucky prisoner ate the pie!

Yet, with God's help Adoniram triumphed over the dreary idleness, the downright physical torture of the twenty-one months he rotted in Burmese prisons, for he saw it all as God working in Burma in a magnificent, mysterious way. "Gouger, this war is going to turn out to the advancement of the kingdom. Here I have been ten years preaching the Gospel to timid listeners who wish to embrace truth and dare not," he said. "And beseeching the emperor to grant liberty of conscience . . . and now . . . God opens the way by leading a *Christian nation* to subdue the enemy!"

In January Ann came no more to the prison with food. Adoniram knew why. Her absence meant their third child had been born! Not a doctor attended Ann; not a midwife in town spoke English!

One day late in January the guard jerked his head toward the door. Creeping toward it, Adoniram saw a beautiful woman in Burmese dress, her hair drawn tightly back, fastened with a white blossom, her orange vest flowing open like a kimono to show off a crimson silk skirt. But she was no dark-skinned Burmese; she was his Ann!

And she was healthy and alive. She held out to him a puny, squawling baby, his Maria!

Months dragged by. Weakened by heat, breathing germ-ladened air night and day, Adoniram contracted tropic fever. Ann, on her rounds of calls to charm the governor, begged for permission to build a little shack on the government enclosure close to the prison. Here she could at least bring Adoniram his meals, nurse him part of every day.

The governor, enchanted by the American teacher in Burmese dress, permitted it. And in a scrawny little bamboo shack, Adoniram and Ann spent two or three precious hours together each day.

One morning as Ann bustled about setting Adoniram's breakfast in front of him, the governor's messenger interrupted. The governor commanded Mrs. Judson's presence immediately. It was hardly an unusual request; her visits had been so frequent. Ann followed the messenger. Perhaps this was the good word they'd waited for so long!

When she was scarcely out of sight, rough prison guards stormed into the shack. Stamping on furniture and walls like so many enraged jungle beasts, they smashed everything in sight. Then they fell on Adoniram, ripping the clothes off his back, dragging him out of the prison yard to the courthouse.

There, in a forlorn cluster stood every white prisoner from the Hand-Shrink-Not, roped together in pairs. Guards pushed Adoniram into line, tied him fast to Captain Laird. The grim-faced *lamine-woon* mounted his horse and gave the order. "March!"

Barefoot, Adoniram stumbled along, reeling from fever and hot sun.

"Where to?" he hissed. Nobody knew. They suspected this meant a quick execution in some lonely spot.

What would become of Ann? She mustn't follow him. It would do no good.

And his Bible, guarded so cautiously all these months! Was some guard right this very minute ripping that pillow to pieces, kicking the pages gleefully around the prison yard?

Chapter Ten

THE LONG TORTURE

IT WAS A MACABRE PARADE. Roped together, the white men shuffled along in pairs, clad only in dirty, tattered shirts and underwear. Their shoes were yanked away by the snickering guards; before Adoniram marched even half a mile, the sand ground his feet to a bleeding, blistered pulp. Hats were snatched too, and the sun burned down on their defenseless scalps. Sometimes staggering, sometimes catching back a helpless moan, the desolate little band inched along toward Aungbinle. Bringing up the rear was the arrogant *lamine-woon*, shaded by a huge hat, smugly astride the only horse!

After they limped along for about four miles, Adoniram's grim determination to bear even this torture melted. He could stand no more. Pitifully, he begged the *lamine-woon* to let him ride awhile. He pointed to his feet, one mass of blood and raw flesh. The look that the *lamine-woon* tossed him was full of a brown man's contempt for a weaker, more stupid, white man!

Did it humiliate Adoniram to turn to Captain Laird, roped to him, and ask if he might lean on his shoulder the rest of the way, to ease a little of the weight from his feet? Captain Laird, a robust, man, agreed. They started off.

Captain Laird's robustness petered out quickly with

the added burden of the limping missionary. Again Adoniram stumbled along on his own. Just before he toppled over with exhaustion, Gouger's Bengali servant joined the ranks.

He whipped off his own headdress, ripped it in two. No use to ask the heartless *lamine-woon* to stop. As he walked, Adoniram bound first one bleeding foot, then the other, with the ragged headdress, hardly stopping his stride. The Bengali lent Adoniram his strong shoulder.

But the *lamine-woon* had no desire to carry dead prisoners the rest of the way by cart; he decreed that the parade would halt for the night. He herded the men into a falling-down shed. Food? Did the prisoners dare ask for luxuries? He slammed the door in their faces. If the wife of the *lamine-woon* had not been curious and a little pitying, as she peered in at the white men, they might have all starved that night. She went away and presently came back with fruit and sugar and a few tamarinds.

By noon the next day this incredible march from Ava was over. The white men stared hopelessly at what was their destination. After all this, they arrived at another death prison, the death house at Aungbinle.

The prison looked as if it were ready for death indeed. The bamboo walls were rotting and sagging; there was hardly any roof left at all. Prisoners could not be housed in this abandoned, decrepit place, but they *could* be burned alive.

Before Adoniram and the others railed out against their fate, or composed their minds for the inevitable, the Burmese workmen swarmed over the prison. They patched walls; they mended the roof. This prison was not to be destroyed and the men with it. They were to be housed here, kept alive in some manner for some time at least.

There was another surprise for Adoniram. Still tied to Captain Laird, he heard a soft voice calling him in English. It was Ann—alive, smiling at him as if they were standing in the mission garden.

She had snatched up the two-months-old baby Maria, her two adopted Burmese girls, implored a servant to come along too, and had made the long trip from Ava partly by boat, partly in a jolting oxcart.

Adoniram looked at her in dismay. "Why did you come! You can't live here!" he rasped out. She would surely be killed; there was no place to house her here.

But as usual, Ann had her way. She stayed. With her cleverness and her sweet smile, she found even a place to live. The prison guard himself offered her one of the two rooms in his cramped house. There, in a dirty back room used partly for storing old grain, Ann settled down with her little brood. And the day after she arrived, one of the Burmese girls came down with a fever that meant only one thing—smallpox!

The horrors of Aungbinle were no less than Ava's death house. Adoniram's bones were weary with waiting for release. His mind tramped impatiently ahead, fretting about the work he was not doing, wondering about the fate of his Bible manuscript. Six more months dragged out mercilessly.

Ann escaped the smallpox. (She had been vaccinated before she left the States.) But she could not escape the terrible tropic germ that struck her down, left her miserable, weak, and thin. She struggled back to Ava for her precious medicine, returned hardly able to walk, and toppled into bed, half-dead, for the next two months with pain and utter fatigue. Only the Bengali servant nursed her.

But to the stricken band of prisoners came a faint gleam of hope. The pakan-*woon*, bitterest enemy of foreigners, had been convicted of treason and promptly executed. His highhandedness had ordered the white prisoners removed from Ava. They learned that he had shipped them to this remote village for slaughtering, so that he might witness the spectacle in the proper atmosphere! But now he was dead! Could this mean that their sufferings were to be cut short?

In November, 1825, a full six months after the men had stumbled up the hot road from Ava, a courier knocked at the door of Ann's shack. In his hand he held a letter from the governor. Adoniram Judson was, indeed, a free man.

Hastily Ann packed their few belongings. She would meet Adoniram in front of the jail and—. But freedom was not to be so easy or so soon.

The stubborn, evil Aungbinle jailer stood obstinately in the way. "Mr. Judson is free, ah, yes, quite true. But the governor does not mention Mrs. Judson."

"But—but—" Ann protested. "This is silly. I never was a prisoner. I came here because I wanted to. You can't hold me."

The jailer shook his head. "The governor does not say even one word about Mrs. Judson."

It took a full day of frantic pleading and the very

reluctant gift of every bit of food they had left before both Adoniram and Ann could start for Ava.

When they parted that night, Ann to go back to the deserted mission house on the river bank, and Adoniram to report to the courthouse, it was an easy good-bye. For the first time in almost two years, they had nothing to fear, nothing to regret when they parted. They would be together in the morning—for good.

But the next time Adoniram saw Ann, it was again from the dirty floor of the Ava death house. The smiling jailer made it all so clear. There had been a slight mistake. Mr. Judson was not to go free at all. His services were much desired by the Burmese government; he was to be shipped upstream to act as interpreter in the British peace negotiations. He would, until his duties were over, remain in chains, of course.

They allowed him about ten minutes to stop at his home, kiss Ann good-bye, pack a very few clothes, and start out for the British-Burmese peace talk.

The translating went slowly. Adoniram, dizzy with fever, endured hour after hour of British demands, Burmese reluctance. Finally, officials decided he need help no more. The delirium, result of the fever, hindered coherent translation.

"We have no further use of him," they ordered. "Return him to the Golden City."

But the Burmese were not through yet. Coming back into the city of Ava, Adoniram limped directly past his house. Only a weak light glimmered from under the door. He begged, bribed, cajoled, teased the guards to let him stop. Just for one moment. Woodenly, they repeated the official command: take him to the court-house.

He spent the night crouched in an ancient out-build-ing. The next morning, he faced the officer in the courthouse.

"From what place was he sent to the peace treaty?" The presiding officer looked bored.

"From Aungbinle," was the answer.

"Then take him back!"

Waiting shipment to Aungbinle, he was boarded up in an out-of-the-way shed. It was in this shed late that night that Moung Ing, the doggedly faithful Burmese convert, discovered him.

"How is she?" Adoniram repeated over and over.

"She longs to see you."

"But how is she?"

"And she entreats you to appeal to the governor, just one time more."

"But how is she?"

"She longs to see you. This will tell you how she is— just the same."

After the Burman had sneaked out into the shadows, Adoniram realized his answers had been sheer evasive-ness. Something wrong with Ann! Moung Ing, his eyes darting everywhere but to the teacher's face, had not said—directly—that she was even alive!

Surprisingly, the fat, jovial governor came to Adoni-ram's rescue. He was released in the morning.

On maimed ankles that wobbled and shook, Adoniram tried to hurry down the Ava streets. For the first time in two years he was going to walk into the house, a free man. He was going home to Ann.

Or was he? Frantic with worry, he half-stumbled up the street, and in through the open door. Crouching in the ashes of a long-dead fire, shaking her head mournfully over a pan of coals, was a grimy half-naked Burmese woman. In her arms was a puny baby, skin and hair matted with layers of dirt. Adoniram brushed past the two.

Lying across the foot of the bed as if she had fallen there, was a woman—as thin a woman as Adoniram had ever seen. Her mouth was pinched as if she had been trying too long to hold back a groan, her cheeks were gray and gaunt. He came closer.

Her head was covered by a dingy coarse cotton cap; it looked as if she had no hair. Could this possibly be his Ann?

Chapter Eleven

AFTER THIRTEEN YEARS —
A NEW BEGINNING

THE WOMAN OPENED HER EYES as if she were lifting a heavy weight.

"Ann!"

In a jumble she told him the story. She had been sick again, very sick. In a kind of half-delirium she remembered Dr. Price shaving off her curls, blistering her head. She pointed to the filthy cap and tried to smile. She was certain that only this had saved her life. What happened after that, she couldn't quite remember.

She tried to say something more, lifting her hand and pointing vaguely toward the table.

To satisfy her whim, he crossed the room. There on the rickety table was a bundle of old parchment. It was—yes, it was—his Bible. He hugged the pages to him. He counted them. Not eaten by worms, not ripped up by a guard, his Bible, his ten years of eye-strain and headache—was all safe!

"But how—"

He pieced together the story. Exactly as he had suspected, the jailer had ripped open the pillow the day he marched from Ava. He tore off the outside matting and flung it to the ground. But he was a fussy fellow. He was not to be beguiled into taking a hard pillow, just because the white man thought it suitable for sleeping. Down in the mud went the lumpy stuffing, the cotton bag containing the precious translation. Next day, Moung Ing, snooping about the crushed bamboo hut for any relics of the revered white teacher, came across his pillow. He carried it, not aware of the treasure inside, to Ann!

The Burmese Bible was saved!

On February 24, 1826, the last signature was inked on the British Burmese treaty. Officials dismissed Adoniram as interpreter.

But they had one more singular request of him. They asked him to accept a permanent position as British interpreter. They named a flattering salary and pointed out all the advantages in government work—protection, security for his family, no persecution.

Adoniram turned down the offer. "This one thing I do: preach Christ. I have no time to make money," he added. Back in Braintree, Massachusetts, he had dreamed about the fastest way to fame and wealth; now he turned the British government down flatly. He had work to do in Rangoon; this was his dream now.

He awoke from that dream into a harsh reality when he landed in Rangoon on March 21, 1826. His mission was broken and scattered. He had left a snug little home, a flourishing native church of eighteen converts, missionaries trained to carry on his work. But the house was decayed and sagging, the missionaries had fled to Calcutta during the war, and of his hard-fought-for converts, only four remained—Moung Ing, Moung Shwaba, and the two women. The others had been killed or scattered. Buddhism had lured back two.

He faced the shocking truth. He had struggled for almost thirteen years; he had endured two years of imprisonment for this mission. Now that mission simply did not exist.

Building again in Rangoon was senseless. The city was under British rule only temporarily. When the Burmese took the reins, anything might happen. The old despotic tyranny would have many new grudges against a white skin. Chaos had taken over in the city itself. Tigers ran wild in the streets, making off with dogs, even children, for food. Families buried their dead every day; famine haunted everyone.

But abandoning the mission at Rangoon did not mean he deserted the Burmese people. Exactly the opposite! In prison he felt certain God was using a Christian nation—Britain—to redeem in a round-about-way a heathen nation. He was sure of it now.

During the fighting, Tenasserim, part of seacoast Burma, had become a brand-new British protectorate. People living there spoke Burmese, were Burmans, in fact. And every day more and more men and women sneaked out of Ava and out of Rangoon to crowd into this territory that reveled in true freedom. Adoniram declared he would open his new mission there—in the city of Amherst, only a plot of high land boldly overlooking the sea, but sure to grow into a thriving city in a few years. The British general himself promised to make Amherst his headquarters.

On July 2, 1826, Adoniram, Ann, and the four faithful converts landed in Amherst. They tackled the new work with zest.

But the British government was not through with Adoniram. Now Britain wanted to negotiate a commercial treaty with the Burman king. Civil Commissioner

Crawford begged him to join the embassy staff temporarily. His knowledge of the delicate nuances and shadings of the intricate language was needed desperately.

Refusing at first, one intriguing angle tantalized him. Crawford promised to throw in his weight for a religious liberty clause! Adoniram could not resist.

He and Ann said good-bye almost cheerfully.

"Only three months at the most," he promised.

"Three months of being treated like royalty—best accommodations, finest food! Oh, Don, how can we complain about that after all we've been through."

"You *will* keep busy?"

Ann smiled. "Now and then. Let's see, there's my school to start and my Sunday services to hold, and two schoolhouses to build. And oh, yes, I forgot, our house to build too!"

But the work for the government was more tedious, more frustrating than he expected. He chafed at spending idle hours this way, wasting his eyes on translating such purely commercial trivialty when he might be home finishing his translation of God's Word. And the religious clause! The promise had been a hoax. The Burmese were no more in the mood for religious liberty than they had ever been.

In November a black-sealed letter was cautiously laid in his hand. So little Maria had gone home to Heaven he thought. Then he ripped open the seal.

"My dear Sir: to one who has suffered so much, and with such exemplary fortitude, there needs but little preface to tell a tale of distress. It were cruel indeed to torture you with doubt and suspense. To sum up the unhappy tidings in a few words, *Mrs. Judson is no more!*"

Chapter Twelve

THE HOPEA TREE AND
THE JUNGLE GRAVE

H E RETURNED TO AMHERST, of course. He sailed into
harbor on a bleak January day. Roger Wade met
him at the dock, and together the two missionaries
paced the path from the harbor to the mission house.
A lonesome wail, like the sound of wind in the jungle
trees, followed them along the path; villagers ran from
their bamboo shacks and lined the path, crying out
loud for the great sorrow of the white man.

At the door of the mission house, Adoniram stopped.
It seemed as if surely Ann would dart out to kiss him
hello. But when the door opened, Wade's young wife
stood there instead. In her arms she held a scrawny
youngster, a little girl who twisted her gaunt little face
away from Adoniram and cried when he tried to touch
her. This was Maria Judson, Ann and Adoniram's two-
year-old daughter.

After a while he went along to Ann's small grave,
high on an embankment overlooking the thrashing sea.
A crude fence outlined the grave, uncovered by any
grass yet, and over it hung a wistful, graceful hopea
tree. "Tree of hope," Adoniram thought, without bitter-
ness. He walked on reluctantly to stand by the house
where he had left Ann, staring at the very spot where
he had stood when he kissed her good-bye. Presently,
he went back to the mission house and the Wades.

They told him the whole sad, bitter story. How Ann had died alone except for one nurse borrowed from a British schooner in the bay. For two whole months after Adoniram left, she supervised the Burmese workmen with zest. A schoolhouse for Moung Ing had been hammered together, then one for her own classes, finally a house.

Early in October her old trouble, fever and dysentery, had doubled her with pain, left her burning one day, trembling with chills the next. From the first she knew she would die. The British doctor did all he could. The kindly European nurse stayed with her night and day. But Ann, who had lost a baby at sea, given birth to another without a midwife, jolted feverishly from Ava to Aungbinle in an open cart, had never known anything quite so terrible as this pain.

"The teacher is long in coming," she moaned to the nurse. "Tell the teacher that it was—" she struggled with the words, "most violent. I am not afraid of death but—but I am afraid I shall not be able to bear these pains!"

It was too much of an effort to talk. For two days she lay almost motionless, her arm under her head, her eyes squeezed shut. With a sharp gasp she called out in Burmese a sudden, almost involuntary cry of painful distress. Ann Hasseltine Judson was dead at thirty-seven, just fourteen years after she had been married in the west room of the New England homestead.

Losing Ann was too incredible, too monstrous—for a man just released from two years in a death house. Adoniram had no strength to react normally. Like Ann, he almost lost his sanity.

He plunged immediately into the work of the mission;

he tensed himself against slackening his pace even for a week or a day. As the others watched in helpless horror, he imposed upon himself a rigid discipline of fanatical asceticism!

The missionary who brought the sparkle of Boston's dry wit to mission tables, who reveled in quick repartee over coffee cups, withdrew. His conversation was glum and to the point of the matter at hand. When he was not working with them, Adoniram left the other missionaries entirely alone. He did not live with them, even in sight of them. Instead, he built himself a bamboo hermitage far out in the jungle, close to the haunt of the wild tigers.

In back of the hermitage he dug a grave. Nights he sat at the grave's edge and imagined himself in it. Here he tried to conquer his fear of the physical nastiness of what happened after a human body was buried.

Had he ever really won the old battle with ambition? Austerely, he drew himself away from any chance for fame. He set out to destroy everything that might tempt men, either while he lived or after he died, to honor him. He wrote a curt letter to Brown University, rejecting the honorary doctorate they had already conferred on him five years before. He ripped to pieces or burned letters from British officials, congratulating him for wartime interpreting; he destroyed some unique translations of Burmese poetry. When his sister in Massachusetts asked him to sign and return a legal document, he refused until she gave him her word that she had done away with all but four or five of his mission field letters.

This same twist of mind nagged him into getting rid

of every penny he had saved through years of pain-staking, petty thrifts. With a single stroke he transferred it all to the mission. And when the British government paid him more than two thousand dollars for his war-time work as interpreter, he turned around and laid the check on the desk of the mission treasurer!

Squatting at the edge of the grave he had dug for himself, he teetered on the edge of sanity, too. While he was still trapped in his own despair and discourage-ment, disaster struck again. The missionaries opened the grave beneath the hopea tree a second time, and Adoni-ram buried little Maria, who died just six months after Ann, his third child to die in Burma!

Was it the next disappointment, not quite so person-al, but no less tragic, that pulled him back to sanity? The Amherst mission was faltering badly! Less than a year after Ann's death, Adoniram could say flatly that Amherst, the town they'd sailed into with such high hopes, had been the worst choice possible. They'd been guaranteed that it would be the shining new metropolis of the strip of British Burma, Tenasserim. Those specu-lations had been wrong! The British general had hon-ored, instead of Amherst, Moulmein, as his headquarters. And Moulmein was twenty-five miles to the north. In 1827 while Amherst was still a little town of two thou-sand, straggling along the high embankment, Moulmein bustled with an impressive river frontage and a popu-lation of nearly thirty thousand!

Adoniram's next step was dramatic and highly typi-cal! He sent George and Sarah Boardman, a young missionary couple recently arrived from America, and the Wades scurrying up to Moulmein to begin a new work; he stayed behind long enough to lock up the mission house, say a last good-bye to the grave beneath the hopea tree. Then in Moulmein with Moung Ing, the faithful convert, the rest of the little flock of converts from Amherst and Rangoon, and seventeen young girl scholars, he placed his feet squarely and began preaching the Gospel.

Heartbreakingly, it meant beginning at the very beginning again. Adoniram built a *zayat,* not nearly as grand as the one in Rangoon. It was a little shed that jutted out into one of the filthiest streets in the whole town, a street where the racket was incessant and distracting. Here he taught every day. Out in the country he threw together another *zayat,* and across the town, a third, where Moung Ing read the Scriptures to his countrymen every day. George Boardman opened a school for boys; Sarah and Mrs. Wade taught an enthusiastic little handful of Burmese girls.

Then suddenly there were more converts than ever before. They flocked to the *zayats;* they stayed late to question and to accept. The schoolhouse overflowed. Adoniram had been in Burma sixteen years and, at last, the work began to move!

He even found time for his translating! Before leaving Amherst he had delved into his Old Testament translation. But he had stuck on the New; his "lust for finishing" as he mocked it, for perfection, had plagued him. But in Moulmein he finished up the New Testament, completed much of the Old, and put into simple Burmese a dozen or so tracts that made salvation and the Gospel clear. And these were no mere story-tracts; they bore such astoundingly learned titles as "The Golden

Balance, or the Christian and the Buddhist Systems Compared."

Yet, Adoniram was not altogether happy. He was strangely restless. He had come to penetrate the depths of Burma with the Gospel, and he was tired of pretending that a few outstations on the outskirts of British Burma satisfied him! He looked around at the missionaries huddled together in the Moulmein mission, grunting his disapproval in a letter home. With millions dying and going to Hell, eight women did the work of two in Moulmein!

And curious news was leaking back from Rangoon. Tha-e, a native convert who wandered off during the war, reappeared and announced that all this time he had been preaching the Gospel of Christ! Now he had gathered enough converts to rebuild the church in Rangoon. Adoniram ordained him, the first Burmese pastor, and sped him on his way. The thought of a strong church in the city he had prayed for so long tempted Adoniram right back into the heart of what he still called the "real Burma."

He watched Sarah and George Boardman pack their belongings to leave Moulmein for Tavoy. In this inland city, still under the British flag, they took the Gospel to the wild and ignorant Karens, in untamed jungle land. The Wades shipped out to Rangoon in February, and in 1830, when a printer, Brother Bennett, arrived from America, Adoniram set him to work at the Moulmein station and promptly booked passage back to the city where he and Ann had first lived!

Landing at Rangoon with the pleasant memory of the Moulmein success, he had no inkling that his attempt to invade the darkness of the "real Burma" was going to end in failure, blocked by his old enemy, court disapproval, and a new one—sheer inefficiency on the part of his own missionary staff! He considered Rangoon only a stepping stone. He planned to pierce the blackness of interior Burma by sailing farther up the river to Prome, to preach the Good News in a city that had been founded hundreds of years before Christ, yet had never heard the Gospel!

In Prome he settled at the foot of the towering idol, Shway Landau. In a tumbledown, gone-to-seed *zayat* he preached and handed out his tracts recklessly to anyone who could read. The people were curious and friendly. Some confessed Christ.

But one morning the *zayat* was empty. He walked down the streets, and the dogs snarled at him. Their masters stood by and snickered. Two small boys flung a handful of street filth on his clean suit. The next day the *zayat* was still empty. He found out why. The king at Ava, the new ruler on the great Golden Throne, was furious at his attempt to smuggle a new religion into the very heart of his empire. Adoniram sadly prepared to retreat.

Too late he learned this rumor was totally false. Actually, the king was more than mildly curious when he heard about the enterprising American missionary. Wistfully, he decided his own staff could benefit by some religion.

"Why does he not come here to Ava?" the king inquired. "He is a good man. If he were here, he might teach and discipline my ministers. He might make better men of them!"

But the ministers did not want to be better men. It was they who spread the rumor, who beguiled the Prome citizens into believing the king would punish if they listened to the American teacher!

"Afloat on my own little boat, I take leave of Prome," Adoniram wrote, sailing dolefully toward Rangoon. "I take leave of Prome and her towering god Shway Landau, at whose base I've labored for the last three months. Too firmly founded art thou, old pile, to be overthrown just at present—but the children of those who now plaster thee with gold will yet pull thee down, nor leave one brick upon another!"

If he had to retreat, it would be by inches. He stopped at Rangoon, determined to work until he was chased. And here to his astonishment he found a changed folk, receptive, eager, openly seeking. The Burmese converts had their own phrase for it: "their ears are thinner!"

He had never had an audience like this for either his sermons or his tracts. To everyone who could read, he joyously handed a tract, sometimes two, and perhaps a portion of the translated Scripture. Still the villagers flocked in, more than a hundred a week!

But one morning Adoniram made a startling and discouraging discovery. His cupboard of tracts was practically bare. He had left only about twenty copies of the "The Golden Balance," that clear cut comparison between Christ and Buddha, and he doled these out like "drops of heart's blood," he said ironically. Frantically, he posted a request for tracts to Brother Bennett, the Moulmein printer. Would brother Bennett please *hurry!*

Chapter Thirteen

A BIBLE FOR THE BURMESE

BUT THE PRINTER BUNGLED! When the bundle of printed matter arrived at last from Moulmein, Adoniram ripped it open excitedly. Out fell two bundles of brief two-page Scripture extracts—exactly what he did not want!

There was only one thing Adoniram loathed more than clutter and dirt—inefficiency. To the meticulous man who could put his hand immediately on any paper in his study without lighting a light, this mistake was inexcusable. He wrote out his exasperation to Brother Bennett.

"Six weeks have elapsed since I wrote for 'The Golden Balance'! I am glad that the 'Epitome' is printed, but after all we shall not give away one a week of the article. Of 'The Golden Balance' I shall give away one hundred a week!"

He waited impatiently for the next ocean freight. Rangoon's festival time—a mad, mardi-gras sort of holiday—crowded him. Ten thousand people or more would jam the swamp streets of the city. Rich men from China, scholars from Siam, families from upstream jungle villages, young men and old men from all over the East would flock into Rangoon in a holiday mood. Brother Bennett *must* understand.

But Brother Bennett remained obstinately obtuse. Another great bundle of paper arrived. Adoniram pulled open its wrappings and sat back with a groan. Still Bennett had not sent "The Golden Balance," that delicately worded tract contrasting Buddha and Christ so effectively. He had stuffed the package instead with "A Catechism of Astronomy," not even remotely suited to Rangoon's carnival frame of mind.

And Brother Bennett had tampered with the translation, attempting to improve a little here and there. Improve! Adoniram shuddered at the crudities he had used in his ignorance.

He wrote once more. "Only contrast the face of one who has astronomy forced upon him with another who seizes the 'Balance,' gloats over the picture on the cover, and goes away almost screaming and jumping for joy." Festival time was almost here. Would Brother Bennett ship back ten thousand of the tracts at once!

Eventually, with all the maddening slowness of the Burmese transportation, "The Golden Balance" arrived. On one-half of them Brother Bennett had omitted the cover picture!

In sarcasm Adoniram whipped back, "I suppose you cannot clap the picture on the cover of those that do not have it now," he wrote sarcastically. "It doubles the value."

In exasperated despair the missionary wrote, "If you listened to me before—fine. But if I were to repeat my request again with all the urgency of a dying man, it would be no use, I suppose!"

Yet the tracts arrived before February's end, festival time. And the curious flocked in.

There was a saffron-skinned scholar from Siam. "Sir, we hear there is an eternal Hell. We are afraid of it."

There was a sweet-faced youth from Kathay in his magenta robes. "Sir, we have seen writing that tells about an eternal God. Are you the man who gives them away?"

"Are you Jesus Christ's man?"

"Give us a writing that tells about Jesus Christ."

And the same missionary who had been so astonished when God gave him a single convert after six years of struggle, now preached through his written tracts to more than ten thousand Burmese! And he gave tracts only to those who asked for them.

Did Adoniram think now God had planted his mission securely in Burma? That his problems and sufferings and trials and sicknesses were all over? It must have seemed that way. Plodding along at his translation, he finished Genesis, much of Exodus, Psalms, Song of Solomon, Isaiah, and Daniel this same year. And when the Baptist mission board in America invited him to furlough in the States, he rejected his chance for a long vacation. He said later he never watched a ship sail out of port for England or America without wanting to jump aboard. But his letter to the board was quite definite; his health, though poor in past years, was much improved. He had far too many irons in the fire to let them cool. He wanted to stay in Burma. And yet—at that time—he had not been in the United States for eighteen years!

Those days as he worked, he must have sung to himself a great, glad song. It was a song of God's blessing, long delayed. But swelling up and almost drowning it out, for a while at least, was a crashing chord in the minor key. On a preaching trip through the tangled paths of the Karen jungles, George Boardman, the mission's righthand man, had died. Sarah, his twenty-eight-year old wife, was left with a three-year-old child in the desolate country.

Adoniram hadn't forgotten Ann's death, his own terrifying sorrow. He sat down and wrote immediately to young Sarah. "Take the bitter cup with both hands and sit down to your repast. You will soon learn a secret—that there is sweetness at the bottom!"

Thoughtful, considerate Adoniram meant the letter merely as a comforting gesture from someone who had known sorrow. He did not even suspect then that he and Sarah would very soon comfort each other in their extreme loneliness.

Later that same year, 1831, you would have seen a slight man in a black suit striding along the river front highway in Moulmein. His copper-hair glinted in the hot Burmese sun. He walked with the purposeful stride of someone who walked a lot (he had taken morning walks every day in Burma) and who had a goal in mind (he had returned to Moulmein to take over the reins of the mission work).

What he found at Moulmein delighted him. Affairs were going extraordinarily well. The rollbooks listed many new Burman, Karen, Taling converts—all baptized into the Christian faith. The timid, elusive Karens had been persuaded to abandon their nomadic living to settle in villages, so that the missionaries might build churches for them! At the end of that year, 1831, reports declared one hundred and seventy-six baptized at Moulmein, seventy-six at Tavoy, and even five back at Rangoon. The work shot up as fast as a jungle plant that blooms between sunset and sunrise.

Adoniram's next decision was difficult and distasteful. Relinquishing most of the active preaching, he gritted his teeth to concentrate on the translating that had already taken such a toll of his eyes and his health. Chatting with intelligent inquirers in the *zayat* was far more palatable, but he dedicated himself to finish the job.

This was his reason. He was the only man alive who could do it! In a cramped room attached to the mission chapel he closeted himself. Studying and sleeping here, he ventured out very little during a day—for his early morning walk, for two meals, for his walk after sunset. On occasional evenings he lingered to chat with other missionary families.

It must have seemed as if the weary missionary had dug himself into these quarters to dedicate the rest of his life to the work. "I consider it the work of a whole man's life to produce a really good translation of even the New Testament in an untried language." He had written it himself in a letter to the mission board.

But the translating barely inched along. He was hampered, first, by his own fussiness. He set up a schedule of a mere twenty-five or thirty verses a day. He refused to make what he mocked as a "second-hand" translation. He worked from the original Greek and the original Hebrew directly into Burmese. And he did not parcel out the work to willing converts. They might blur the fine shadings. He determined to do the entire work firsthand himself.

It was his "lust for finishing," as he termed it, that

desire to polish and polish until every sentence glowed, that hamstrung him. Convinced that his New Testament was still imperfect (he had been working on it then for almost twenty years), he set out to revise, just one more time. Then he re-did the entire Book of Psalms. He looked wistfully back into the Old Testament.

"As to the Old, I am not well satisfied. The historical books are pretty well done, but the poetical and prophetical books are doubtless susceptible to much improvement, not merely in point of style, but in the rendering of difficult passages."

If he thought he had buried himself in the musty study to finish his work and his life alone, he was quite mistaken. When he chose to escape the mustiness by exploring deep into Karen jungle country, it was something more than the air along the Salwen River, more than the fascination of visiting the jungle people with the Gospel, that sent him back to Moulmein with a new spring in his step!

How he liked to preach to the Karens! They listened so well, they understood so easily. Thanks to a hoary legend handed around tribal fires for centuries, they believed that a white messenger would come by sea to teach them. Anything this white-faced teacher said, they listened to respectfully.

A bearded chieftain invited Adoniram into his own hut for worship and prayer, promised that he would follow the new religion and lead his people in the way. A woman, bedecked with fancy beads and who professed to be a Christian, heard thoughtfully Adoniram's scolding about simple dress, then laid every glittering ornament at his feet. A dark-skinned husband and wife accepted Christ, insisting they must follow Adoniram through the slippery, crooked jungle paths until he reached a stream for proper baptism. An arrogant chief exiled them to preach in a tumbledown shack; before the meeting was over, he himself crossed over the line from Buddha to Christ. One night Adoniram baptized nineteen converts.

But most fascinating of all about the craggy Karen jungles was the courageous white woman who preached Christ there. Sarah Boardman, hardly more than thirty, had turned down all insistences from the States that she return. Even friends who argued about little George's health were refused. Taking the little boy with her, she climbed mountains, forded streams, plodded through marshes, cut paths through the jungle in all kinds of weather.

And this was the kind of courage Adoniram admired. It was the kind of high courage Ann had possessed. It was exactly the kind of courage that Adoniram demanded from any woman with whom he might possibly fall in love. Just when he did fall in love with the quiet, motherly, home-loving girl from the hills of New Hampshire is not exactly recorded.

On April 10, 1834, three years after the death of George Boardman, eight years after the grave beneath the hopea tree had been dug, Adoniram Judson and Sarah were married. She was fifteen years younger than he.

They went directly back to Moulmein. Adoniram plodded along at his translating, while Sarah gently domesticated the missionary.

Their home cost only three hundred dollars, but it

was extraordinarily happy. Along the front were three rooms, with two smaller rooms behind, and a detached kitchen. A wide veranda ran the full length of the house. The disturbance and the danger and the stark tragedy that stalked his years with Ann had made impossible a quiet home life. With Sarah it was different.

He now read in the mornings. Before noon he preached in the public *zayat* to anyone who wandered in. In the afternoons he translated or read proof on his Bible. In the evenings he conducted worship in the mission chapel. During these years, Abby Ann was born, then Adoniram, Jr., then Elnathan. Life became very peaceful.

In 1839 he was exactly one year short of handing to the printer his very last page of the Burmese Bible. In spite of his nagging hunt for perfection, he was almost ready to admit that the job was done. He strained over the final polishing of his New Testament revision, and then his work was unexpectedly cut short.

Exactly when the Burman work had taken root, when he was about to finish a task that had taken twenty-two years of his life, Adoniram's health shattered. No mere eye-strain, nor even the dysentery—this was a sharp pain that clutched his throat and threatened to choke him.

"Nothing, nothing at all. Just a cough and throat ache." He pushed away Sarah's motherly care.

"The doctors don't say so. Your medicines don't help you any more. And listen to you, husky as a London foghorn."

"You've let those doctors frighten you."

"Yes, I have. Enough so I'm insisting you forget

about me and the youngsters and get some good, fresh, cool sea air in your lungs."

"It's not my lungs. It's my throat. I told the doctors."

"And they told you. It might be your throat, but it still could be *tuberculosis*."

In February, 1839, Adoniram packed his still unfinished manuscript and sailed out of Moulmein on a ship heading across the bay to Calcutta. In the end he had listened to Sarah and to the doctors who told him frankly that his only chance was a quick escape to sea air, and that this was only a very slim chance!

Chapter Fourteen

THE TEDIOUS DICTIONARY

T UBERCULOSIS OR NOT Adoniram made up his mind
before he lost sight of the Burman coasts, he'd waste
no time in Calcutta! Of course, it was pleasant to be
greeted so genially by the English Baptists there. Of
course, it was soul-satisfying to take tea in a gracious
home, enjoy cultured, witty conversation. He stayed
just three weeks, convinced when he left that the annoying little throat irritation was cured for good. Tuberculosis, indeed!

On shipboard he happily discovered a Burman convert. Some of his old energies bounced back. He wanted
to prove to himself that the Judson voice hadn't lost
its old resounding ring. He invited the delighted native
into his cabin for a Sunday morning worship service.

It was a small cabin, and Adoniram and the intent
Burman huddled close enough for conversation. Open-
ing his Burmese Bible, Adoniram read from it. Then
he began to preach. The sermon was short, and Adoniram hardly lifted his voice above a conversational pitch.
It shouldn't have been any strain.

But by mid-afternoon that day Adoniram found out
just how much of a strain it had been. Almost before
the Burman left his cabin, he began to cough. In the
afternoon his fever shot up. He lay helpless in his cabin,

fever scorching his skin, the cough rasping at his voice. Did he wonder then if he had preached his very last sermon?

Back in Moulmein he admitted against his will he was no better. The other missionaries watched dejectedly as the witty, talkative spark plug of their whole enterprise sat silent at meeting time, even at meals. Someone suggested another sea voyage. Adoniram put the suggestion away. Timidly another mentioned a trip to the States, perhaps a whole year's visit. Adoniram looked his scorn.

But he stopped bragging about the fitness of his lungs. He began to hear stories about other missionaries who had died of tuberculosis that ravaged their throats. Utterly miserable, he slumped over his study table, unable to get his translation copy ready for the printer.

He no longer railed against being plucked out of the heart of his work, when he was hardly fifty-one, when he saw the whole thing taking shape. He was intent now only on holding on until he finished the translation. If he could only down the pain, with what medicine was available so he could drag along—he must finish the Burmese Bible!

Then in October after ten full months of miserable silence, Adoniram mounted the pulpit in the native chapel. As the Burmans and the missionaries crowded around, eager, waiting, some of them tense with concern, Adoniram raised his voice to God again without a cough or a quaver. The sermon was unusually short for a man who always found so much to say about the Gospel. His voice was so low that the men in the back leaned forward a little to hear. But Adoniram Judson had preached again!

A year later, in October 4, 1840, he laid down his quill with a flourish and called to the mission printer. At last he had finished his translation into Burmese of the entire Bible, from Genesis to Revelation. He revised, edited, changed, or perfected no more. He finished exactly twenty-three years after he had begun. The two pages of Matthew, handed out to the first Burmese convert, had grown into a voluminous, bulky book. The manuscript that had been buried in a garden, kicked around a prison courtyard, salvaged through Ann's bravery and a convert's faithfulness, was ready for the Burmese people. From his fussiness and his frustrating precision, he created a book with its words so right in every shading that it still stands today as the best Burmese Bible in existence.

Almost before he could sit back and stretch, Adoniram faced another serious problem. Sarah was sick. The old chronic dysentery that had pestered her when she first arrived in Burma, returned with its knifing stomach pain, its nausea, its high fever. Married five years to Adoniram, she had had four children. This had not helped. In desperation Adoniram bundled Sarah and the youngsters (they were ailing too) into a ship bound for Calcutta.

They set out in high hopes, not knowing how miserably the health trip would fail. Cooled by strong sea breezes, the youngsters, Sarah, and even Adoniram himself brightened before they reached Calcutta. There they settled into what was recommended as a "high, dry house" by the missionaries in Serampore. The house was dry, true—dry because the sun scorched it that way. Adoniram, the blue-eyed patient Sarah, and all the youngsters had quick, complete relapses.

Henry, a rolypoly little boy not yet two, was sickest of all. Less than three weeks after they landed, he died.

When a kindly sea captain volunteered passage on his ship back to Moulmein, the Judsons accepted. That he charted his passage by way of Port Louis, through the treacherous Bay of Bengal, could not be helped.

The trip was disastrous. August storms spewed up the thrashing waters of the bay. Squalls smashed the ship's top mast, the top gallant and the jib boom. Sarah, expecting her fifth child, sat up sleepless night after night. In December they limped into Moulmein, after an absence of almost six months.

Returning with them was an old enemy, Adoniram's throat and voice inflamation. Even low-pitched conversation hurt. Adoniram knew he might never preach in Burma—or anywhere else—again.

But was that any reason for the mission board to dump on him its most disagreeable task?

"Compile a dictionary? I will not! I set them straight years ago!" Adoniram stormed to placid Sarah. "I will not squander my hours when there are so many other—"

"That's what you said then," Sarah agreed.

"Exactly. I even recall the words. 'In regard to a dictionary, I do not see how I can possibly undertake. Must the population of twenty thousand be left to perish without any effort to save them, except what is made by a very few inefficient native assistants? Ought there not to be a *preaching* missionary—' "

"That was *then*," Sarah insisted.

"And it's true. This country needs preaching. Not a musty old dictionary. At least not by a missionary."

Sarah regarded him steadily with her clear, blue eyes. "And *you* can't give them that preaching. Not now. But the dictionary—"

Incredible as it seemed to Adoniram, Sarah was right. His voice that had boomed out across the Rangoon highway from the *zayat* veranda was husky, sometimes unintelligible. To speak out loud exhausted him with pain.

And so in 1841 he drew his chair up to his desk to outline a Burmese-English dictionary. Though he loathed the job, thought it barren and sterile, he lavished on it all his fanatical meticulousness. He formulated an elaborate time schedule. If he labored steadily every day, he could complete the dictionary in about four years—by 1845. Some might race through it pell-mell, but he shrugged off such speed as shoddy workmanship.

Slowly he collected his data, enlisted a few highly literate natives. He outlined the dictionary in two parts— Burmese to English, English to Burmese—and settled down to his job.

He poked through the first letter in the Burmese alphabet, tackled the second.

In December, 1843, little Charles, doomed to be an invalid all his brief life, was born. Barely, a year later, Edward was born. He was Sarah's eleventh child; three were born when George Boardman was alive; in ten years she and Adoniram had eight. Now doctors shook their heads, agreeing pessimistically that if Sarah were to survive her chronic dysentery, a trip was imperative —not to Calcutta, but to the States.

The dictionary! Adoniram's days now revolved around it. Late at night, oil lamps flickered as he tussled with obscure Burmese synonyms. The mission board had convinced him that future missionaries desperately needed this aid. A trip to the United States meant a delay of two, even three years. Without his assistants, he'd be bogged down in confusion. No one in the States knew the language well enough to help.

Then why not take his assistants with him? He coaxed two, a government writer from Rangoon and the intelligent nephew of a high court premier, to board the American-bound ship with him in May, 1845.

Into his cabin Adoniram lugged papers, books, quills, unfinished manuscripts, old Burmese books. He planned to allot hours every day to the work, on ship and in the States. Burmese servants carried Sarah aboard, the three older youngsters tagged afterwards, while the others waved good-bye from the docks.

Out of the harbor and in spite of rugged storms, Sarah seemed perkier. When the ship sprang a leak and made for the Isle of France, she announced her brave little decision.

"I'm going on alone."

"Insane! I won't let you." Adoniram's husky whisper only emphasized the words.

"I'm so much better. You go back and spend the time working. You'll get so much more done in Moulmein.

"Yes, but—"

"Send your assistants back right away. With them off, you'll be sure to go too."

Sarah persisted, showing him a scrap of paper on which she had scribbled a poem:

We part on this green islet, Love,
Thou for the eastern main,
I for the setting sun, Love—
Oh, when to meet again?

My heart is sad for thee, Love,
For lone thy way will be;
And oft thy tears will fall, Love,
For thy children and for me.

Yet my spirit clings to thee, Love,
Thy soul remains with me.
And oft we'll hold communion sweet,
O'er the dark and distant sea.

Then gird thine armor on, Love,
Nor faint thou by the way,
Till Buddh' shall fall, and Burmans sons
Shall own Messiah's sway.

Adoniram admitted she seemed better. Repacking his manuscripts, his papers, Adoniram commissioned his two assistants back to Moulmein. He planned to follow them up the coast in a few days.

Almost before they were out of sight, Adoniram turned back to Sarah. Shocked, he saw she was worse, much worse. She murmured a little when he told her he would not let her go on alone. He would go to America, exactly as he had planned in the beginning.

But as he stood watching her, he realized his two assistants were merrily heading up the coast toward Moulmein. There was no chance in the world of catching or even communicating with them. He—and his dictionary—were headed for America without them, and they were to have been his only possible help in all the western world!

Chapter Fifteen

WHISPERING THUNDER

COLD WINDS BRUSHED the "Sophie Walker" as she curved around the Cape of Good Hope, and Sarah propped herself up and ate heartily. But the cold winds were only a temporary blessing, and while the mid-Atlantic island of St. Helena was still just a dot on the captain's chart, Sarah slumped again. When the ship anchored in the island port, Adoniram knew Sarah would never again see her parents in New Hampshire nor her oldest son in his Worcester school.

In the tight little cabin, Adoniram leaned toward her, stroking her hand. She was so sick, her beautiful blue eyes blurred, bloodshot, her thoughts meandering confusedly in a dozen directions.

"Be sure Abby has her clean dress before you dock. Promise me you won't speak a word out loud at any meeting when you get there. No matter who asks. And little Charlie, tell the nurse—"

Adoniram gripped her hand. That he grated out his words huskily over his inflamed throat made them no less tender.

"Sarah, my dear."

She opened her eyes, tried to focus them on her husband.

"Do you still love the Saviour?"

She spoke coherently, intelligently. "Oh, yes."

Another pause. "Do you still love me?"

She almost smiled, murmured brokenly their special phrase, her own way of telling him that, in spite of their unconventional married life, even if she were dying, she certainly did love him.

"Then give me one more kiss."

She died somewhat before dawn, and they buried her high on rocky St. Helena. It was a forlorn band of people who stood in the cemetery that afternoon. The four bewildered little Judson children, in their ill-fitting mourning clothes, borrowed at the last minute by the ship's captain, and their gaunt, sallow father who talked, when he spoke at all, in a muffled clumsy voice.

The ship waited neither for tears nor nostalgia. The next day it put out to sea, and Adoniram stood sternward, yearningly looking back at the rocky promontory, remembering his graves—Rangoon, Amherst, Serampore, Moulmein, St. Helena.

Another shock waited for the exhausted missionary when he completed the journey that seemed like a senseless, frustrating delay. The new democracy, just a baby when he left, had grown up!

Gliding into Boston Harbor, the "Sophie Walker" threaded her way between commercial ships that flew the flags of half a hundred nations around the world. And the streets of Boston—why, the New York he had explored in his twenties had not been so crowded, so busy. And breathing a choking kind of soot into the air was a curious new invention called the railway car. Was this the same country he cherished so long in his memory!

Even more shocking was the flattery, the congratulations. He had expected to rest obscurely in comfortable New England. Instead, he was astonished to discover that people everywhere knew his name, were waiting to applaud his story!

At first he refused to speak to a single audience. His throat was damaged irreparably by the pulmonary disorder. To talk above a whisper was agony. His doctors had ordered him not to speak anywhere, under any condition. And besides, he added with a pathetic little smile, he had promised Sarah he wouldn't. But there was another reason, one that hardly anyone suspected.

Thirty-three years ago, he had made a tremendous sacrifice; he had forfeited the English language. He made his choice when he determined to *think* Burmese. Since then he had not spoken in a public meeting in his own tongue. Before an audience, he could not put more than three sentences together in English. This yellow-skinned, weary missionary was more truly Burman than American.

But the good church folk of this country were not to be robbed. They *must* hear him. And they came forward with a solution. Let Adoniram Judson speak in Burmese, and let him *whisper* if he must. They would place an interpreter at his elbow to catch every syllable and repeat it aloud in English.

So, the second night after he arrived in Boston, he was rushed to the city's Bowdoin Square church. As he whispered his greetings in Burmese, someone interpreted hesitantly. "I beg your prayers for the brethren I have left in Burma, for the feeble church I have planted there, and that the good work of God's grace—"

A man was running down the aisle. The translator

stumbled, then stopped. The church folk turned their heads in annoyance. What would the eminent Dr. Judson say to this peculiar interruption?

But the man—he was about fifty and respectably dressed—ran straight toward the platform. As the audience watched aghast, he leaped up on it. Suddenly Adoniram jumped to his feet. The two men were in each other's arms, crying, laughing, trying to talk all at the same time.

For the man who dashed so unceremoniously down that aisle was Samuel Nott, the only survivor, except Adoniram himself, of the handful of young seminary students who had dared to revolutionize Baptist and Congregational thinking about foreign missions!

Thus began Adoniram's round-the-country junket. Many were startled to discover that the bold young man of Andover, of whom they'd heard so many legends, was a mere wisp of a man, with a weary face and voice. But disappointing them even more was what he said.

One minister put it bluntly. "Brother Judson, I trust you'll understand me. After your meeting tonight—Well, sir, to tell you the truth, the folks were expecting— They wanted a *story*."

"That's exactly what I gave them," Adoniram replied. "Most thrilling story I can imagine, the story of salvation."

"But they've heard that before. What they wanted from a man who has just come from the netherlands of Christianity—"

Adoniram broke in impatiently. "My business is to preach the Gospel of Christ. Not to tickle their fancies with amusing stories, however decently strung together

on a thread of religion! Tell me—how could I—in the
hereafter, I mean—face God's charge: 'I gave you one
opportunity to tell them of me. You spent it painting
your own adventures.'"

Throughout his stay in the States, Adoniram felt
strangely out of place. There was this matter of the
railroad trains. He had never ridden one in his life.
In Worcester one day he boarded a Boston-bound train,
properly settled the matter of his ticket, and sat back
to enjoy the trip. Was he comparing the comfort of
his plush seat with the portable chair that carried him
those aching miles between Masulipatam and Madras?

When a young teen-ager tapped him on the shoulder
and held out a newspaper, Adoniram took it, smiled
his thanks and unfolded the paper. As he skimmed the
headlines, the boy watched him gravely, not moving
on. The stranger in the next seat squirmed uneasily.

"I believe the young fellow's waiting for his money,"
she prodded.

Startled, Adoniram fumbled for his wallet. "Been dis-
tributing papers free so long in Burma," he mumbled,
embarrassed, "I never expected anybody'd want money
for them."

But if the famous missionary was slightly more eccen-
tric and considerably less prepossessing than they expected, the people of America found out quickly he
had lost none of the fury of his fight for the Gospel!
At the Baptist mission society's triennial convention—
a convention that had heaped praise and flattery on him
—Adoniram anticipated a great doxology for God's blessing on foreign missions.

But instead, discussion was gloomy. Dignitaries complained about the heavy debt. One minister suggested an incredible remedy: close down a mission station. He named one specifically, Arracan.

But Arracan was on the Burman coast! Adoniram ignored the fact that these were the same men who had honored and extolled him a few hours before. Jumping to his feet, he pounded on the pew for attention. The words growled from his throat as he forgot the doctors' cautions.

"I must say a few words. I must!" Amazed that he was speaking English, stunned at the sound of his voice—pitched above a whisper for the first time in front of an American audience—everyone listened. "I protest against the closing of the Arracan mission!"

Dramatically, he dropped back into the Burmese. "If this convention can do without my dictionary, and I think it can, I'll go to Arracan myself. At once! And if you must have the dictionary, I'll go as soon as it's done," he was whispering now, "if I live that long. I'll go to Arracan to work there and die—and be buried there."

He had saved Arracan! Unanimously, the convention voted to keep the mission open, not with their senior missionary's help, but even without it.

Three months later Adoniram interrupted his cross-country tour to visit an old friend, Dr. Gillette, living in Philadelphia. On the trip to Philadelphia Dr. Gillette handed him a little book titled *Trippings*. He recommended it for light reading on the boring train ride. And for the second time Adoniram Judson's life was to be radically changed by a book!

Actually, *Trippings* was a very frivolous little thing. He skimmed it quickly.

"The woman who wrote this is intelligent," he judged. "Too bad she wastes her talent on such froth. A woman who writes so well ought to write on better subjects."

Dr. Gillette smiled. "Tell her yourself. She happens to be a guest at my house right now. You'll meet her tomorrow."

The next morning Adoniram was introduced to Miss Emily Chubbuck, a pert young woman with wide-set eyes and a quick smile. Thinking only of her writing, he sat down with her on Gillette's overstuffed sofa.

Emily looked up at the famous missionary from Burma expectantly. Adoniram looked back unsmiling. "Tell me," he said huskily, "how can you bear to use your talents as you do!"

Chapter Sixteen

ONLY TWENTY RUPEES
FOR RANGOON

SIX MONTHS LATER, June 2, 1846, Adoniram Judson, fifty-eight, and Emily Chubbuck, twenty-eight, were married.

That day in the Gillette's living-room Emily had retorted to his criticisms with a forthrightness he admired. Why did she misuse her talents? Her answer was one frank word: money, money that she needed badly.

She was being truthful, not flippant. Her father had alternately hawked newspapers and farmed; he failed at both. The Chubbuck home was a miserable ramshackle cottage, a sieve in a snowstorm. When as an eleven-year-old she hired out to the local wool factory, her earnings, all of a dollar and twenty-five cents a week, bought groceries.

She was teaching school when an editor discovered her lighthearted, conversational writing had a kind of magic in it. Disguised by the pen name, Fanny Forrester, Emily had written ever since, supporting herself and her mother and father.

There was nothing frivolous about this intelligent young woman author. Critics had compared her with Emily Brontë and Elizabeth Barrett Browning. Probing even deeper, Adoniram found a keenly religious woman. At the age of eight she was truly converted. In her

118

teens, impressed by a missionary biography, she wistfully hankered for the mission field. The book was, incidentally, the tale of Ann Hasseltine Judson!

But the Judson-Chubbuck wedding pleased no one at all. Literary critics, so generous about Fanny Forester's writings, were not nearly so generous about the December-May marriage. Their frank opinion: Fanny's ridiculously throwing herself away on that old missionary.

Respectable Baptists, dignified clergy, heavy contributors to missions looked the other way in embarrassment. The venerable founder of American missions marrying for the third time, a mere chit of a girl, and a writer of light fiction at that!

Adoniram and Emily ignored the raised eyebrows. In mid-July, six weeks after the wedding, they boarded a Burma-bound ship. It was the hardest good-bye of all. Adoniram knew very well he had seen his friends for the very last time. His four oldest children he had settled in American schools. And on the Boston dock, waving until the ship disappeared, was a strapping young fellow of eighteen—George Boardman, Sarah's boy.

The trip to Moulmein must have been full of old memories for Adoniram. In mid-Atlantic they sailed under the shadow of St. Helena's rocky cliff cemetery. Straight past the Isle of France they sailed, where Adoniram and Ann had looked so mournfully down at Harriet Newell's grave. Running along the coast of Burma, at last, Adoniram took a telescope to peer up at Amherst's green promontory where Ann was buried. In Moulmein he hugged Eddy and Henry to him as he introduced Emily, but little invalid Charlie was missing. He had

died exactly one week after Adoniram and Sarah sailed
for the States.

In Moulmein Adoniram might have settled down to
a smug domesticity with his lighthearted, pretty, young
bride, his two sons, and of course, his long-delayed
dictionary. But instead, he determined to try once more
in his lifetime to see Rangoon brought to Christ. Old!
Not he! He mustered every bit of strength left for one
last dramatic attempt to pierce the darkness of "true
Burma." Besides, in Rangoon scholars to help on his
dictionary were plentiful.

Two and a half months after he arrived in Moulmein,
he packed his dictionary manuscripts; with Emily and
the boys he sailed toward Rangoon. Ahead lay disappointment far more tragic, far more heartbreaking than
the death house imprisonment, than the stubbornness
of the great Golden One. Ahead lay a terrible anti-
climax to his lifetime of bravery and sacrifice.

He entered the city not as missionary, nor as a "pro-
pagator of religion," but simply as a priest and a minister.
The governor granted him permission to minister only
to foreigners settled in Rangoon.

The present great Golden One in Ava not only dis-
liked missionaries, he was a roaring, fanatical Buddhist
bigot! If Adoniram were caught proselyting even once
the remedy would be quick and simple—banishment,
or even death!

Making a showy display of all his dictionary work,
openly advertising his need for scholarly translators,
Adoniram surreptitiously began to preach. He patched
together the old Rangoon native church. One by one
Burmans heard that the missionary would tell them

about eternal life—if they came to him quietly, anonymously after dark.

Almost imperceptibly the little church began to grow again. He and Emily moved into an immense, unhealthy brick house in the heart of the dirty, smelly city. It was a house with no glass windows, with huge barren rooms, a house Emily promptly dubbed "Bat Castle." In one evening she and Adoniram hunted down and killed two hundred and fifty bats. Moving in and keeping house with them were the mosquitoes, beetles, cockroaches, spiders, lizards, rats, ants—and an unnamed species, black and big as the end of Emily's little finger.

Distressing news drifted in from Moulmein. A flash fire had burned all their valuables and their good clothes in storage there.

The rainy season drizzled down, and the Buddhist Lent starved them. Emily could buy no meat in the market-place and only a half-rotten fish now and then. For weeks they lived on boiled rice and fruit. One youngster was in bed with erysipelas, the other with a variety of undiagnosed ailments. Emily was so weak from sheer lack of food that her legs buckled under her if she tried to cross the room. Dysentery kept Adoniram away from his translation for six weeks.

Then, as the cluster of native Christians grew stronger, the great Golden One on the throne in Ava laughed long and mockingly in the face of the American missionaries. He stationed a police guard directly outside the Judson home with instructions to strong-arm every single Burman who left the house unless that Burman could prove that he was a legitimate family servant.

With worship services scheduled the very next day, two dozen or more Burmans would be slipping innocently into the Judson gate. Frantically, Adoniram dispatched his own servants to make the rounds of the Christian homes in Rangoon. He was defeated—forced to cancel his own Sunday worship.

"Don't you see, Emily, they've beaten us. Unless, unless—"

"Unless what?"

"Unless we storm right into Ava and beg the great Golden One himself for some decent tolerance! What have we to lose?"

Emily hesitated. "But if we failed, Adoniram? We could be banished, couldn't we?"

"And have to leave our pitifully few clothes and pots and pans behind?" Adoniram shrugged. "What of it?"

Emily quietly studied her hands. "Could he—the great Golden One, I mean—throw us in jail?"

"And we'd stay just as long as it takes to get news to Moulmein. This isn't 1820, Emily. Things have changed since—since those days."

"But he could say 'off with their heads.' He could, couldn't he?"

Adoniram was not impressed. "We have to die sometime, don't we? Emily, you've convinced me! It's the only hope for Burma."

"You mean—"

"A trip to Ava. Immediately!"

The time did seem right. The governor in Rangoon gave his permission with no delay. A friend of Adoniram's served in a high place in the Ava court.

The irony of what happened next made it all the

more tragic. Adoniram's petition for religious tolerance in Burma was solidly blocked by a most unexpected opposition, his own mission board.

A letter from Moulmein crushed his dream. Unbelieving, he read the news. There was simply no money to pay for his trip up the Irrawaddy. The mission in America had slashed the budget by ten thousand rupees, not below last year's budget, but below actually running costs.

"I thought they loved me," Adoniram mourned to Emily. "And here they weren't even thinking about me."

For his month's rent of eighty-six rupees, Moulmein headquarters posted him only a meager twenty. Not only was his trip to Ava absolutely out of the question, but he did not have the funds to stay any longer in Rangoon.

He retreated to Moulmein a discouraged man. Gritting his teeth, he settled down to his Burmese dictionary again, the only job the mission seemed to have a heart-interest in. His throat inflammation still plaguing him, he preached little.

But the growing native church was a pleasant balm. Every month missionaries baptized Burmese, Karens, Talings, and in 1849 there were fifteen hundred baptized members of the Burman church in the Moulmein mission. In the Arracan mission there were twice that many!

In December, 1847, little Emily Frances was born. Though Adoniram fretted about his wife's health that next year, he wrote home in 1848, "We are a very happy family. Not a happier one, I'm sure, on the whole broad earth!"

Amazing news came the next year from America.

After all these months the mission board had reconsidered his plan to go to Ava. If he wished, he might leave at once. Belatedly, they granted him an allotment of one hundred rupees to pay his expenses.

Chapter Seventeen

"SUCH GLITTERING PROSPECTS"

BUT THE INVITATION came too late. He had already bargained with a Moulmein scholar for final help with his dictionary. He did not dare to slow his pace; nobody else could ever decipher his scribbled notes!

And four months later—he was gone.

At the end of 1849 he completed the first part of his mammoth dictionary, the English-Burmese section. This was a prodigious piece of work, a volume of six hundred pages that took him almost ten years to complete. And no one but he could have produced it. No one in all Burma, either Burman or foreigner, knew the intricacies of both languages so well.

Although he never considered the dictionary one-tenth as important as his Bible, he knew it was labor well spent. He realized it would help all who labored after him in Burma. But he never guessed that same dictionary would be the core of all Burman language study—one hundred years later!

Nor did he guess, when he finished the first part and began the second, that his lifework was almost over. In September, 1849, helping Emily with the babies one damp night, he caught cold.

In less than a week the cold crept down to his lungs.

His fever shot up, the cough tore at him. After that, the dysentery.

Frightened by his history of tuberculosis, Moulmein doctors dared lose no time. They advised an immediate sea voyage along the Burma coast. Weakly Adoniram submitted.

When he and Emily returned, no one saw any improvement. The doctors could only recommend another dose of the same cure. In February, the Judsons sailed for Amherst.

But in Amherst he was isolated with no medical help. Every day he grew weaker. When he walked, he tottered, clinging to furniture and the walls if he thought Emily were in the garden. His face was as pale, as yellowish as the Burma moon. Even the rainy season, usually a benediction of coolness, only steamed him.

In panic Emily wrote to the Moulmein mission station. The missionaries there sent an urgent request: Judson must come home.

Back in Moulmein he no longer tried to walk from room to room. He lay on the couch and disconsolately watched his feet swell. Sometimes he slept fitfully for twenty-four hours at a time. When he talked, it was about the past—Andover, Rangoon in the early days, the Bayonne jail.

As Emily puttered in his room one night, he shook off the smothering lethargy. When he spoke, his voice rang with the old commanding note.

"This will never do. You're killing yourself for me. I'll not permit it."

Emily studied him gravely. "But it's only for a little while."

He knew exactly what she meant. "That doesn't distress me. Not the way it did. Maybe I'm too weak."

"Why should it distress you? You—with such glittering prospects ahead!"

Adoniram opened his eyes. "I do not believe I am going to die. I need this illness, Emily. I'll recover and be a better man."

"You want to get well?"

"Want to! Emily! The dictionary's only half done. And all our plans—"

"They think you won't." She was whispering.

He twisted his head sharply toward her. "I suppose they think I'm an old man—that it's nothing to give up this old life that's seen so many trials. I'm not old. You know I'm not. No one ever left this world with—brighter hopes or—warmer feelings." He sighed. "Don't be afraid. Death won't surprise me. In spite of what I say. I feel so strong in Him."

Now he balanced precariously between life and death. But fresh sea air might swing that balance—if he could reach it in time.

The French bark "Aristide Marie" in the Moulmein harbor agreed to take the sick man aboard. (She was bound for the Isle of France, that island of so many memories.) To get him to sea as fast as possible was imperative. Sailing the very next day was a government troopship, and the civil commissioner ordered this ship to tow the bark out of the river. Weeping Burmans carried Adoniram aboard.

But the military commander of the troopship rebelled on the very morning of the sailing day! He refused to take orders from the civil commissioner.

The two men argued and dickered—for twelve hours, twenty-four hours, two, three, four days. And in his stifling cabin, Adoniram weakened. Still the sailing delayed. Not until five days later did the ship move down the river and out into the bay.

It was too late. That very day his pain tripled, his left side swelled ominously. Wednesday he slept all day and ate nothing. On Thursday he did not try to drink even water.

Friday morning—it was April 12, 1850—he turned wearily to his Burmese servant. "It is done." He called out in the Burmese, "Take care of poor mistress." At a quarter after four he died.

Dressing him in the black suit he always wore, they buried him at sea. There was no funeral service. Through the larboard port they lowered him silently into the waves.

In Malden, Massachusetts, an unimpressive marble tablet tells the story:

> IN MEMORIAM
> Rev. Adoniram Judson
> Born August 9, 1788
> Died April 12, 1850
> Malden his birthplace,
> The ocean his sepulchre,
> Converted Burmans and
> The Burman Bible
> His monument.
> His record is on High.